Whatever Next?

PAM WEAVER

Pam Weaver

DEDICATION

I would like to dedicate this book to my beloved husband, friend and soul mate Dal, our fantastic children who make us so proud, and our eight gorgeous grandchildren who will make sure we never really die. Also to all of our many friends who, over the years, have stood by us through thick and thin. Also to Eileen and Gabrielle who had such faith in my ability to write this book.

Pam Weaver

CONTENTS

Pam Weaver

ACKNOWLEDGMENTS

My thanks go to Eileen, not only for all of her help in the creation of this book, but for her friendship over the years I have known her.

Pam Weaver

FOREWORD

I've known Pam for about 38 years. She was a great friend of my father's and was always at the farm when I was a young lad. I remember she borrowed a Dexter bull from my dad Joe, who founded the Cotswold Farm Park. Dad always kept Dexters because, being small cattle, they were very popular with the visitors to the park. Pam also bought a red Dexter bull from Dad called "Farmpark Raynard" She went on to show him very successfully. Pam's a proper country woman and a true ambassador for the Dexter Breed Society.

As one who's done it, I can assure you it is quite a task to write a book about yourself and Pam has completed the job with her usual honesty and openness.

If asked to describe Pam I'd have to say that what you see is what you get and this, too, is so very true of this, her first book.

Adam Henson (Countryfile)

Pam Weaver

FROM THE AUTHOR

Writing this book has been a real pleasure. It was something I had thought about doing for a long time. Anyone who knows me would never have dreamt that I would have done it. I always think of myself as an ordinary person but I do have a fascinating story to tell.

I have done many talks for local W.I. groups and at the end of each talk, ladies would come over to me, saying how much they had enjoyed my talks. They would say "You should write a book". Well, it all came about out of the blue. I booked a cruise for six weeks, leaving England in January this year (2018). Never had I done such a long cruise as I am a full-time cattle farmer, but the animals were all in for the winter and my two sons agreed to look after everything while I was away.

I was allocated a table of six in the restaurant and we all got on very well and did lots of talking. After about a week they started saying, "Pam, you really must write a book," to which I said, "People have been telling me that for years but I really don't have the time." "Well," they said, "you have the time now.

You could do it in the next five weeks." So the seed was planted and the next morning I started writing on scraps of paper. We were at sea for a couple of days and when I was able to go ashore the first thing I did was buy a writing book and I was away. Writing seemed very difficult at first but it soon got much easier and by the end of the six weeks I had written 30,000 words. I was so pleased with myself. I had only written on the days at sea, sitting on the deck in the shade because, gosh, it was too hot in the sun. I have enjoyed writing about my life. I hope you find it enjoyable and hope it will encourage you to have a go. It's a lovely legacy to leave your family.

CHILDHOOD

1. PAMELA JEAN PENSOM

I was born November 1942 at Huntley Hill, Gloucestershire, the middle one of three children and the only daughter.

I had two brothers, Burton, six years older, and Roger, eight years younger.

My Mother, Dolly Rose, was a wonderful person, loved and respected by everyone. In my whole lifetime I have never heard anyone speak against her. She loved her boys which I came to accept. From a very early age I used to think I was there for their convenience but that was not surprising because my mother was the eldest daughter of a gentleman farmer (William Nelmes).

Grandmother Fanny

Her own mother, Fanny, had died in childbirth when Mum was five years old. She had a younger sister, Muriel, and her father remarried an older widow with three older children. Mum was always her stepmother's skivvy. She had to get up in the morning, light the range and have the kettle boiling before her father got up, fetch fresh milk from the cowman and have his breakfast on. She was not allowed to go to work to earn her own money. She was kept at home to run the house and help out in the fields.

Mum preparing to milk the cows

My father's father, Nathaniel, was a castrator of animals and that was stated on my father's birth certificate.

I was born in the same house as my dad, Horace, and maybe in the same bedstead. I know it was known that my mum had married below her status but I guess it was a lot to do with getting away from her life as a skivvy.

My parents were hard working country folk. We lived off the land and had a pig that was killed in the winter months. That was the only time the boys had a football to kick around. It was the pig's bladder which was blown up. After two days it was in a foul state and the smell would keep you running from it. It would then develop a hole and, thankfully, go flat.

A family photo at Burton's christening

Looking back, I know that I had the most

incredible childhood. Money was short but we ate really well. My dad was an excellent poacher and taught me well. He had poacher's pockets sewn into his jacket and living on the edge of woodland, there was always something to shoot or catch with a ferret. I loved to go with him and I soon learned to never talk and be careful of my footing so not to tread on a dead branch as it would crack and make too much noise if I did.

2. DEEP FILLING

Deep Filling was a lovely little community of five cottages, the Hart's house and our house. The cottages belonged to Herbert Knight who owned the land. Some of his workers lived in these cottages. There were about ten or twelve children, most of which went to Huntley school. On summer evenings, the older children would meet up down in the plum orchard and use a circle of trees to play rounders. If the game was going really well we would still be there after dark and we would light a fire in the centre so we could see each other. Our parents would come looking for us and would start talking and we would carry on playing.

Above our house was another cottage that belonged to the Acker's Estate along with all of the surrounding woods. They were into timber and had a large timber mill at Huntley. The cottage up in the wood was known as Smokey Bottom. An old lady lived there. I used to go and visit her and one day she took me into the old stone shed and after rummaging around for a while she found an old leather saddle. (I think I must have told her how much I wanted a pony). It was covered in dust and cobwebs but that didn't matter. She gave it to me and said, "Now you have a saddle for when you get your pony". It seemed as if my dream might come true. Sadly, I never did get the pony but I spent hours polishing the saddle and propping it over a log or something similar so I could sit on it and pretend I was riding a pony.

I spent a lot of my summer days up in the woods. I had my favourite spots. I sometimes found dead birds which I would bury and cover with green moss. I would walk to the top of Huntley Hill where there was a clearing with short grass and gorse bushes. This was where I could find Hare Bells which you never see these days. Chick and Hen was another lovely little plant. It grows close to the ground and has a little flower of yellow with touches of brown. I loved to sit amongst them. I could also dig up 'pig nuts'. These grow down from a little white parsley-like flower about two inches deep in the soil and they were nice to eat. I think they were nicknamed 'pig nuts' because the pigs would root them up to eat. I needed a knife to be able to dig for them but I never went out without a knife because I was always cutting something, depending on the time of the year.

There was a well in our garden but I can never remember getting water from it. It was always covered over. Instead, we had to fetch drinking water from a spring, deep in the valley, on the edge of the wood, about half a mile away. Mum and I would make one journey every day. Mum would carry two buckets and I carried one small bucket which, on the return journey, I would keep changing from one hand to the other because it was so heavy. We would stop every now and then to rest, never wasting a drop of the precious water. It was placed in the pantry under the marble slab and definitely only used for drinking. I remember that the washing up water was always put in the pig's bucket. We were never allowed to use any sort of soap in the washing up water because it made nice flavoured drinking water for the pig.

On a Wednesday, every week, as I came home from school, Mr. Thurston would be at our house taking Mum's grocery order. Mr. Thurston had a shop in Newent and the best way of getting our weekly needs was to put an order in. It would be delivered on Friday. Every week he would have a list of special offers for that week, but Mum would keep to her basic needs. He would also run a Christmas club card and, if we could afford it, we would add a little to it each week. We paid a week in arrears for our groceries and he would collect the money from the previous week when he came to take our next week's order, always over a cup of tea. I remember him having a big belly but who wouldn't with all those cups of tea?

We also had an insurance man that called once a month. His name was Mr. Ruscoe. Mum always paid into an insurance. I think it was always known as 'a little nest egg' so maybe insurance on the house.

Way back in my childhood I remember my dad being very friendly with painter and conservationist Peter Scott, son of Antarctic explorer, Captain Scott. It was in the early days when he was first starting up at Slimbridge Wetland Centre. I don't know quite how he and Dad became friends but I always remember he had problems with things killing the birds. We would help him with that and also with the trapping of the water fowl to put rings on their legs. I remember being up in Peter's hide. It was just like a wooden tree house with slits that you could look through. Peter was always sketching and painting in watercolours. We got on really well and he gave me two small watercolour paintings that he had done. I still have them and they bring back more wonderful memories.

My childhood was so magical having a dad like mine. He was also great friends with the estate game keeper Cliff Hyett and we were always up the cherry orchards trying to control the thieving birds. I know the birds that did the most damage to the fruit trees were the bullfinches. They would take the buds in early spring. The bird population in

Pam Weaver

those days was so great that the only way to
protect the crops was with a gun. Cliff and his
wife (Mary, I think) were a lovely couple.
They lived in a little thatched cottage on the
edge of the wood. They didn't have any
children but lots of dogs and proper dog
kennels. They were always pleased to see us
and there was always a lovely cake in the cake
tin. Dad always went home with his poacher's
pockets full and I always left with a few
sweets in my pocket.

When Mum and Dad first got married
Mum came to live with Dad's parents. His
dad rented the house from someone, but over
the years Dad managed to buy the house or at
least started paying for it. I once found an
invoice that showed he was paying monthly
for it. I know it was something like 12s 6d a
month, which in today's currency would be
62p a month. We now look on 62p as
worthless and would not be able to buy a cup
of tea with that, but to my dad that would
have been very hard for him to find each
month, but he managed it one way or another.
Good old Dad.

He was born at Hill View which was sold

12

after my mum died in 1977. I am very friendly with the lovely couple that live there now and often go to visit them. I left Hill View when I got married in 1961. Over the years Hill View has had a few minor changes but is still how I remember it. It's lovely going back home and always being made to feel so welcome by Pat and Charles who love and cherish the house as much as me. Pat and Charles are also best friends with the people who live in Deep Filling where the cider mill used to be and also the couple who live at the end of the drive. Pat and Charles have lovely dinner parties and I am invited and I always end up telling them of how life used to be. We have become the best of friends. It's as if I had never left. There are such nice people in the world and I never cease to marvel at that fact. I feel so honoured to have met so many lovely people.

Me feeding chickens at Hill View

3. GRANDFATHER

My grandfather on my mother's side was a gentleman farmer and proved to be quite a character. He always dressed in a jacket and waistcoat with a gold watch and chain, a cravat tie and stiff white collar. He always carried a walking stick hooked over his arm and wore a trilby hat. He had a wooden cigarette holder for his Players cigarettes and a hankie displayed in his top pocket. He always carried humbugs in his trouser pocket too. We were taught to have a lot of respect for him and only to speak when we were spoken to.

4 generations around the aspidistra at Hinders Farm

I remember visiting him and Nana in the winter evenings. They lived at Hinders Farm which was at the end of Hinders Lane and we lived at the top end of Hinders Lane about a mile away. We used to have really bad winters with sheets of ice covering the lane. Spring water always ran down the lane from Huntley Hill and when it froze we were unable to stand up on it. Once a week, on the same evening every week, Mum and I would make the trip to check on Nana and Grandfather. In the places where the ice was so bad we walked on the grass, holding onto anything we could find to keep us upright. Grandfather still had a cow or two and, therefore, milk for the house. He had a farmhand called George who would milk the cows, so on a winter's evening I was always treated to a bowl of custard made with cream. Nana called it ice cream. Sometimes it was very nice but there were times when it didn't taste so good but I wouldn't dare leave it.

Every Monday Grandfather would go to Gloucester on the bus. Monday was market day and his day out. He would always have a coffee and a cake in the Cadena restaurant served by his favourite waitress. He would always take her one of his best apples which he had polished so much that it looked like wax.

When the snowdrops were out he would get me to pick them and put them in little

bunches which were placed carefully in a basket. He would sell them to Don Meadows' fruit and veg. shop in Westgate Street and he would give me the money earned from the sale of them.

When the plums and apples were ripe, my brother Burton and I would have to go and help Grandfather pick the fruit. I knew Burton was never very happy as Grandfather would make him climb to the top of the ladder for one plum, all the time pointing with his stick. If Burton dropped a plum Grandfather would hit it to the trunk of the tree so Burton didn't tread on it when he came down the ladder. Grandfather would never pick up because, as I said, he was a gentleman and never did any manual work. We would take the plums back to the farm, balancing two boxes on a wooden barrel which had a steel rimmed wheel on it. Back at the farmhouse, plums would be weighed, ready to be collected and so it went on with my brother constantly complaining to me.

4. SCHOOL

School was good and I enjoyed every minute of it. My nick name was smiler.

Our village junior school was Huntley C. of E. It was next to the church and was quite small with only two teachers; Miss Bird, who was headmistress, and Miss Sparrow, who was lovely and rode a bike everywhere. It was an upright bike with a basket on the front and a carrier on the back. Miss Sparrow took the young class. The boiler that heated the radiators was in her room, which gave out fumes from the coke which ran it. I always seemed to have a bad throat from it. I would put my hand over my mouth and would be pleased when playtime came along. After a few years the school had grown and we needed a third teacher, and guess what she was called... Mrs. Gun! Can you believe it? We would say that the Gun was going to shoot the Bird and the Sparrow. That's children for you but in all fairness she was really nice and soon became a firm favourite with us all.

Huntley School circa 1949

We had one girl at school, Kathleen, who was always a mystery. She lived with two old aunties. She was lovely and had long hair done in ringlets, and really nice clothes which came from London. At Christmas time she used to go to parties at Cheltenham Town Hall. These parties were only for the posh children. I remember going with her once as it wasn't much fun for her on her own. I borrowed one of her lovely dresses and some proper party shoes and we took a taxi there. It was fun. I remember the place was very large with big staircases everywhere and very nice carpets. These two aunties, Lily and Florance, lived in a large house up the A40 and along the lane to Ganders Green. It would take about twenty minutes to walk there. In their front room they sold sweets and, if we were lucky enough to have a penny or two to spend, we could go and buy some sweets there. We used to think that Kathleen was very lucky to live there and have sweets whenever she wanted them.

Huntley School circa 1952

I went to secondary school at Abenhall Secondary Modern. This school was on the edge of the Forest of Dean, close to Mitcheldean and about fifteen miles away from home. We were picked up by an old double-decker bus on the A40, Gloucester to Ross-on-Wye road. If you were running a little bit late it was very frustrating because you had to run all the way down to Deep Filling and then you had to climb all the way up the pitch and it just got steeper and steeper. It never paid to be late.

I have very happy memories of school days, especially my junior school. I can remember almost everybody's name and I still have some of my old school photos. I keep saying, when I have time, I'm going to look up my old school friends, before it's too late.

5. MY MATE JACK

I was always animal mad and for a few years I had a pet Jackdaw called Jack. (Well what else would I call him?) He could say his own name! This lovely friend of mine would go everywhere with me, perched on my shoulder.

When I went to catch the bus for school he would come with me. When the bus arrived and I was about to get on he would fly back home and when I got dropped off in the afternoon it wouldn't be long before he was there on my shoulder again.

A day came when Jack wasn't there. To this

day I don't know what happened to him. I was so upset that my beloved Jack had gone but life went on and like my mum was always telling me, "You don't know what's around the corner".

I never tried to replace him because I knew no other Jackdaw would be as good as my Jack.

Jack perched on my shoulder and my cousin Michael

6. LIVING OFF THE LAND

I was often asked to go and catch some rabbits and usually I would take my little brother with me but I remember he was never that keen. I would get the rabbiting bag with all the nets and small wooden mallet in, then go and get one of the ferrets, put her into a small sack and pull the string tight at the top to make sure she couldn't get out. I'd sling the bag over my shoulder and off I'd go. It was always drummed into me to never come home without the ferret.

The next job was to find an area that showed signs of rabbit activity (mainly droppings and, of course, rabbit holes). The rabbit holes I'd cover with nets and secure them by driving wooden pegs into the ground with the mallet. When I was sure I had covered all the holes I would put the ferret down one of the holes, then sit very still on the then empty bag and listen for sounds underground or maybe something moving in the undergrowth. It was always possible I had missed a hole and the ferret could come out. If so, I would catch her and put her back down another hole, then hopefully the next noise would be a squeal from a rabbit as it came rushing out of a hole and into the net. I would run and grab it and kill it quickly then wait for another to pop out. When I had two rabbits it was time to pack up. I would catch the ferret, then pick up the rabbits (never leaving the innards in for too long as they became gassy very quickly). I then collected all the nets, straightened them all out and folded them up individually, ready for the next time. I then went home very proudly with Saturday's dinner.

We always had rabbit and onions done in a large frying pan on Saturdays and, although I was as thin as a rake and a fussy eater, I did like the front legs of the rabbits. On a Monday when I came home from school

Mum always had rabbits' brains on toast ready for me. Just another of my little treats.

An annual task my dad and I would do together was to help the farmers in the spring with sorting out the lambs. They all needed their tails cutting off and the males needed castrating. Only once a year did we get lambs' tails on the menu. The tails were never cut off until lambing had finished so some tails were bigger than others and at the end of the day they were shared amongst the men and they all went home with their sacks of tails.

Preparing lambs' tails so that you can eat them is just about the worst job in the world. Mum would have lit the boiler, the one that was used on Monday wash days, and by the time we got home, the water was almost boiling and she would put a few tails in the water. The secret was not to leave them in too long or, as you were pulling the wool off, the skin would come with it and you would be left with just the grisly bone. She would hold the tail above the water and test whether the wool could be plucked. Dad would also help. There were bits of wool everywhere. They were then put into a bucket of cold water and then it was my job to do the final cleaning and then place them into another bucket. The smell that came from the boiling water was enough to gas you. The pan was soon full of plucked-off wool and the water had turned green-grey. The wool was like a matted carpet on top of the water and, from time to time, taken out with a stick and more water added and so it went on until all the tails were done. Mum and Dad's fingers were all withered up from being in the hot water. Mum would later sit by the fire rubbing a little block of green Snowfire on her hands to try and get some sort of life back into them. Snowfire was her life-line after wash day too. She always made sure she never ran out. As for the lambs' tails, they made a lovely meal, boiled and served with parsley sauce. If you were lucky enough to get a big one you were in for a treat with some meat at the top end. They were so sweet and we would suck every little bone individually. We really enjoyed them because we knew we would have to wait one whole year before we would have some more.

Then there was elver season. As we lived not far from the River Severn we would have the pleasure of eating elvers (baby eels). The

River Severn is the only river in the UK where they come up in the spring tide at high moon. They were very plentiful and cheap or free if you caught them yourself. The most common way of cooking them was in the frying pan with an egg or two scrambled in with them and then sprinkled with pepper and vinegar. Elvering later became a way for local people to earn extra money in the spring time. Men would stay out into the early hours of the morning to catch elvers and sell them to the Elver Station that had been set up to export elvers worldwide. Every spring evening, every car you saw had elver nets on their roof racks. The occupants off to chance their luck at finding the right spot in the river to cast their nets.

Elvers were fished from the river bank. They always kept together like a swarm of bees so it was a matter of just constantly casting the net and hoping for the best. Two mates working close together, about 10ft apart from each other, one would be lucky and bring out net-fulls of elvers and the other man just a few. It was purely pot luck. I never tried it myself, but I think it was the 70s and 80s that a lot of money was made elvering (and tax free). Sadly, there are no elvers now.

Talking about elvers, when we first moved to The Old Mill the brook was full of eels and Martin, then ten years old, spent all of his time in the evenings after school and, of course, helped by Nick (then two years old) eeling. In the beginning they would get one on the end of the fishing line and not have a clue how to get it off so would come running to me for help. An eel is so slippery and slimy and never keeps still so there's a bit of an art to getting them off the hook without hooking yourself. They're very hard to kill, but it had to be done and I had been doing it since I was knee high to a grasshopper. We had a weir on our brook at The Old Mill and during the elver season I actually saw elvers climbing up through the weed to the top of the weir. Our brook flowed to the River Severn so they had travelled all that way up stream against the flow of the water. (Amazing little buggers). We lived quite a long way from the river and our brook winds down through fields and under the canal before it gets to the Severn. Quite a journey for something so small. At Frampton-on-Severn (which, by the way, has the longest green in England) they have always had an elver eating festival. Men would sit at a long table with a plate full of elvers in front of them and the winner would be the man who cleared his plate the quickest. I think they also had to drink a pint of beer.

About twice a year our old pig, that we kept for breeding, would need to be put in-pig and we didn't keep a boar (male pig) so when the time was right, and timing was everything when breeding, Dad would watch for her coming on brimming (that's what you call it when they are coming into season ready for mating). Anyway, when the time was right, Dad would get up at first light and walk her all the way to May Hill to Tony Pritchard, our butcher, who happened to have a boar. Then, when the deed was done, he would walk her all the way back. A lot of the journey was on the main A40 road. Hopefully she would be in pig and we would soon have some babies to sell or barter with.

We killed a pig about once a year, always in the winter, when we were having a cold spell. I can remember having lots of meat everywhere. I remember coming home from school and having to turn the chitterlings (pig intestines) everyday for days. They were in salt water and every day I would turn them inside out on a stick and then put them into clean salt water again. This was to clean them. When they were clean the small ones would get plaited and then all cooked in the boiler. You would eat them cold with pickle and you could keep them for quite a while as long as the weather stayed cold, but I think a lot of them got given away as Dad had lots of brothers and one of them had a large family.

Then of course there was the bacon to salt and cure. This was done on a marble slab and, when finished, wrapped in muslin and hung up on the meat hooks. We had three big hooks coming out of the ceiling at Hill View. Slices where cut off the bacon when needed. There was more fat than lean and the rind was hard with bristles on it but it did smell nice when spitting away in the frying pan. I always remembered it being salty.

My mother was a wonderful cook and could make a meal out of anything. We didn't normally have a pudding during the week and if she didn't have much for the meal (like maybe egg and chips) she would do a pudding and it would be either spotted dick, boiled in a cloth, or steamed jam pudding, served with custard. Lovely!

Sunday would be a roast then apple or plum tart. The butcher, Tony Pritchard, would call on a Saturday with his wicker basket on his arm with a choice of joints from beef, lamb, pork and sometimes veal. There was an old saying that was "never eat pork if there's no 'R' in the month". This was because pork was very hard to keep fresh, so maybe he didn't kill pigs during May, June, July and August.

Sunday afternoon tea was really important. We would have visitors or we would visit friends. The table would be laid with the best table cloth and the best tea set would be brought out and there were always pretty homemade cakes, a trifle and thin slices of bread and butter and then there was Sunday night supper with ham, cheese and homemade chutney.

7. SUNDAY

Sundays were completely taken up with church. I used to go four times a day most Sundays: 8:00am Holy Communion, 10:30am bell ringing for 11:00am Morning Mass, 3:00pm Sunday School and 5:30pm bell ringing for 6:00pm Evensong. Everyone seemed to want to go to Sunday School, possibly because at Christmas we had a party and during the summer holidays we had the Sunday School trip to the seaside. What a treat. No-one wanted to miss that. It was our one and only time we got to see the sea.

My brother took me and my friend Jennifer to Sunday School across the fields. It was a short cut and we always wore our best clothes.

My brother Burton, Jennifer and me ready for Sunday School

Sunday School was on from 3:00pm and we were always back in time for tea.

Eventually I became a Sunday school teacher.

As I grew older I joined the church choir. Not that I was any good at singing (and I knew it) but I would open my mouth and I knew all of the hymns off by heart.

That was also the time I learned to ring the bells. I loved bell ringing. I remember once when I turned up for the bell ringing at evensong, I took my coat off, held onto the sally of the bell rope ready to start and when I looked down I saw I still had my apron on. Oh, I felt so terrible. I had been helping Mum with the washing up then had to rush the mile to church, across the fields. I couldn't be late because I was number one bell and they couldn't start without me. Number one bell is the treble and the lightest bell so not too heavy for me to handle. Anyway, it was too late to do anything about the offending apron until we had finished our peel of bells, then a very red faced me took my apron off and shoved it in my coat pocket. Such a thing would not bother me now but in those days life seemed to have more value for polite and proper things and you didn't wear your apron to church. Your best hat and gloves, yes, but not your apron!

8. MY BABY BROTHER

In 1950 my baby brother was born. I can't remember worrying about whether it would be a girl or boy. I do remember the day he arrived. Dad got into awful trouble because the baby's layette, that was so carefully knitted by my mum, had been placed in the cool top oven to air and because Dad kept the fire going well for the hot water, by the time it was taken out for the baby, it was all scorched a pale brown. I remember my mum being so upset.

I had my baby brother and I absolutely adored him. Mum named him Roger and I wasn't very happy about that because we had a boy at school called Roger and he always had a runny nose and I didn't want my lovely brother to be like that. I wanted him to be called David because there was a lovely boy at school called David. Mum won but I soon got used to it.

Roger was always very much my little brother and I spent quite a lot of time with him. I remember rocking him in my arms to try to get him to go to sleep. I remember thinking my arms would drop off and every time I tried to put him down he would wake up. I was eight years old when he was born and the right age to be a second little mother to him and I adored him.

When he was twelve years old he was going on a school trip to Holland and the school was looking for extra help to go with the children, so I volunteered. I was married by then and expecting my second child. My mum said she would look after my first child, Martin, who was almost a year old, and I went on the school trip with Roger. We had a lovely time and it was a nice break for me. Mum was in her element to have her grandson all to herself for about five days. I remember she didn't want to give him back.

When Roger was seventeen years old he got very much into music and records and soon set himself up as a mobile disc jockey. He had a mate called Rob who had a van, so Rob became his "Roadie" and they started doing gigs with their mobile equipment. They called the outfit POWER TOUCH. The bookings were coming in fast and thick and they needed someone to take the bookings, so his favourite sister got the job. By then we were living at Churcham in our semi-detached, while we were looking for our perfect dream home, but we ended up having two more children and stayed there for five years and, as Roger pointed out, I would be home all day to take the bookings, so I became his manager. POWER TOUCH became very well known in the Gloucestershire area over the next four or five years. After that he decided it was time to move on. He went abroad to work. This was about the same time as we moved to The Old Mill and I was really busy with our new way of life. My little brother had flown the nest.

9. MY BIG BROTHER

My brother, Burton, who was six years older than me always seemed to be out with his play mates. They were never too keen to have me tagging on. I was always told they were doing 'boy things' and to go and see if Jennifer, who lived in the cottage below our house, was coming out to play. Jennifer was not a tomboy like me and we seemed to be always arguing. We always made up the next day though because we both needed a play mate. I remember we used to play hopscotch a lot.

There were days that I was invited to join in with the boys. All of a sudden I had my way and I seemed to be part of their gang but

Jennifer and Me

it would appear that all they wanted was a guinea pig. One such day they had been working on the old apple tree just inside the orchard next to the garden. They had fixed a pulley high over a hanging branch. They had a wooden fruit box attached to it by using a

rope tied to the holes (or handles) in each side of the box. The plan was, because I was small and not very heavy, they would practise hoisting me up into the tree. Everything was going to plan. The box was very lopsided but I was off the ground and rising, with them pulling like mad on the other end of the rope. Then disaster struck. I went careering back down to the floor with the pulley block and most of the rope landing in the box and on top of me. The pulley block had landed on my head and soon blood was trickling down my face.

I never learned my lesson and longed to be part of their gang. I did really have my uses, like when it was time to go apple scrumping. The boys could only get one or two apples in their trouser pockets but I could get maybe ten in my knickers because they had elastic around the legs and the elastic helped to stop the apples from falling out. I had trouble walking though and had to hold my knickers up to stop them falling down. If the farmer came after us then I got left behind and it was impossible to climb over the gate! I remember having nightmares about the farmer coming after me and my legs just not working.

And yet I was still very keen to be one of the boys and longed to be accepted into their gang. Like I have said before, I always had my uses but most days I was told to get lost. Only when it suited them was I allowed to join in.

The brook that ran through Deep Filling came from way up towards May Hill. It came through a wood on the other side of the A40 and had been dammed up by the estate owner and stocked with trout. A trap sluice door had been put in which could control the water in the reservoir. Mr. Warren was the water bailiff and we knew not to let him catch us there, but we worked out that we were quite safe between 1:00pm and 3:00pm. Under the A40 was a tunnel for the brook water coming from the reservoir and it constantly flowed. I was told to stand at the mouth of the tunnel and count the trout that came down. The boys would wedge a strong branch into the lever on the trap door to open it up. It was heavy work and sometimes the stick broke. Also, they always had a lookout up by the road to watch out for the bailiff in case he came along. Finally, when they thought they had achieved their goal they would come and find me, eager to know how many trout had come down. If it was five we knew we had five to find and catch and I became quite the expert at tickling trouts' bellies and guess what... we had trout for tea!

I still loved to get involved with what the boys were getting up to, even after all the trouble I always seemed to get into. Then came that one day when the boys were racing on their dropped handled bikes down Deep Filling pitch and up the other side. I was ten years old now and I could ride a boy's bike with crossbar and dropped handles no problem! John Hart's bike was leaning on the bridge that went over the brook in Deep Filling. I took it and pushed it all the way up

Deep Filling pitch (no-one could ride up there as it was too steep). I got on at the top and tally-ho! I was away. I had rounded the bend at the bottom and that's when I saw my brother coming towards me from the opposite direction, down the hill, again at speed. I don't remember anything else after we collided and my face went into his shoulder. I was out for the count. The doctor came and said I needed rest. My face was a mess. My nose was flat to my face, my lips split. I was put to bed in Mum's bed next to Roger, my baby brother, in his cot. He was two years old now. Mum slept with me and Dad would have been in my bed. I remember my little brother didn't recognise me when he woke up and Mum had to reassure him that it was really me. I couldn't smile or open my mouth any more than to breathe. I certainly couldn't breathe through my nose. After a couple of days the ambulance came and took me to hospital as I couldn't move my head and neck. I slept a lot and would sleep walk. They didn't really find anything that they could treat me for, just saying I had a neck injury and I needed plenty of rest and quiet. Well, I never went to school again for about a year. I always had terrible headaches and kept passing out. The doctor said, given time, I would grow out of it. Mum had a battle to make me eat and so it went on. I missed doing my 11-plus so when it was time to give school a try they had no idea what my ability was as a scholar so they put me in the B-stream. At lunch time I was allowed to walk in the school vegetable garden with a friend, in case I had a black out. I was coping very well. I always loved school and was keen to learn. My favourite lessons were cooking and needlework. By the end of the first year we had our exams and I came top of the class. I was presented with a book, Heidi, which I've still got. It meant I would move up to the A-stream. My headaches got less and I stopped having blackouts, so I was near enough back to normal, whatever that was. I still had a stiff neck which I have to this very day, sixty-five years later.

10. CORONATION

When I was eleven years old the coronation of Queen Elizabeth took place. Everyone in Deep Filling, my aunties and uncles and all of their children came and spent the day at our house because we were the only family to have a television and everyone wanted to watch the Coronation. We all sat around the television very quietly, trying not to miss anything. The large dining table was filled with sandwiches and cakes that everyone had brought with them. The coronation went on for hours and us kids got fidgety and were sent outside.

That night there was a big bonfire on the top of May Hill. Locally May Hill was, and is, a very important landmark. There are said to be ninety-nine pine trees on the top of it and the clump of trees can be seen from miles around. I remember trying to count them but people said that there could never be ninety-nine trees because as soon as they plant the ninety-ninth tree another one dies.

The parishes around May Hill had been busy arranging a bonfire feast on the summit of May Hill, close to the Scots pine trees. The cider mills had been asked to make a special cider for the night's celebrations so we came up with a very strong brew called scrumpy. To me it tasted like vinegar but the men loved it and everyone had a joyous time and the fire burned late into the morning and we went home in daylight.

The cider lorry in the photo has a very big barrel on it and I suspect this was specially made for the coronation and put on the lorry with the special scrumpy brew pumped into it and taken up to May Hill on the night. It would have been tapped from the back end of the lorry and served to all the merry makers, probably with no charge but with everyone expected to bring their own mug.

My dad, as far as I can remember, never drank cider and he always told me not to drink it because there were too many dead rats in it. I believed him, of course, but now, thinking back, it may have been something he said to stop us getting a craving for it. Anyway, it worked and neither me nor my brothers ever drank it.

11. FRUITS OF THE EARTH

My father worked on a fruit estate where they grew apples, pears, blackcurrants and Blaisdon plums. In the summer and autumn those were all harvested by local women and my dad was the one to try and keep them all happy with their allocated lots. It wasn't an easy task as they would be given a row of blackcurrants to pick and there was always one row more heavily cropped than another. My dad could never please everyone. No wonder I only remember him with white hair.

Plum picking was no better for him because it was women and children that did the picking. Dad had to move all their ladders, making sure they were in the trees safely and be able to reach all the plums. Just like the blackcurrants, some rows of trees were better than others. Some trees would be laden with fruit, others hardly worth putting a ladder to, but they all had to be picked. At the end of each day he would go down each row of trees with a tractor and trailer, weigh each of the boxes, which had to be fifty-six pounds. We would be given a ticket for each box of correct weight. When all the pickers had finally gone home and the grumbling had stopped he would take the boxes to the yard and load them on a lorry that would take them to the jam factory.

The same could be said about the blackcurrant picking although with that we sat on a small, low box and buried ourselves into the brush. There were no gaps in a row of bushes so we picked in pairs which meant we never stopped talking and we would try and keep up with each other. The blackcurrants were picked into twelve-pound wooden chip baskets, making sure there was only fruit, no leaves or rubbish. These were taken to the Ribena factory, usually by my dad on the small cider lorry that was used to deliver cider to local pubs. We always had a bottle of Ribena at home which was an unknown luxury within poor families. Apples and pears were ready from September onward. Eating apples and pears were picked by hand and taken to a sorting shed, packed on trays in boxes and put in a cold store. Not something me and Dad had anything to do with. Our domain was the cider mill.

The plum picking gang with my dad in charge

12. CIDER MAKING WITH MY DAD

Fruit was gathered from the orchards in October, brought into the mill and cider making started. The apples were chewed up by a large pulper. This pulp machine was run by a big engine, located in the engine room, which always smelled of oil and hot grease. It had pistons that went up and down and I was told never to get too close. The pulp was then shovelled onto a press, which was a square platform of about four foot square. Hessian sacking was spread on it, which would have been about five foot square. The pulp was then spread on it about two inches thick. The hessian was then folded over to the middle to keep the pulp in place then another sheet of hessian was placed on top of the first one and repeated until you had a stack of pulp layers on the press. The press would then be manually wound down and all the juices would run out. The juice would be caught in a big wooden trough under the press and it was then hand pumped in to the big clean vats. What came out of the press we called musk. It was of no use apart from being fed in small quantities to pigs so it was loaded onto a tractor and trailer and tipped on the edge of the brook to wash away in time.

My childhood was centred around the cider mill. In the winter months I could always be there in two minutes. It was a downhill run into Deep Filling where the old tin, timber and concrete cider mill was running. Alongside was a brook which was constantly used in the mill. The whole of the winter months was taken up with cider. First pressing the fruit, pumping it into great big wooden vats for fermenting, then siphoning off into smaller barrels, ready for tapping. The whole place was filled with the smell of fermenting apples and pears. It was almost like a gas and would take your breath away. It was always lovely to get back out into the fresh air.

Saturday mornings were my favourite time. All the local cider drinkers would come to pick up their week's supply. There were some characters. It was also their favourite day of the week because they could all sit around the old cast iron stove, drinking as much free cider as they liked, trying out all the latest barrels that had been tapped. They brought their bait of a hunk of bread and cheese with them to sup up the cider. The morning ended at twelve noon. Some of them came on bikes with the bottles of cider strapped to the carrier on the back. No-one ever rode away because whatever direction they went in it was an uphill climb and they were in great need of the bike to lean on. One man came in a horse and trap. Dad would help him on board and aim the pony in the right direction and hope for the best. He lived about four miles away. I know he never usually got very far as in the afternoon he could be found along the lane laid by the pony and trap, fast asleep in the grass. The old pony was usually having a nap too.

The cider mill had a lorry to deliver cider to pubs. My dad's pride and joy, a Ford, green in colour with a sign written in yellow. One day a week was delivery day and if there was no school I would go with him. This was a real treat and I would see new places and new people I had not seen before and they always seemed pleased to meet me, saying, "so you are Horace's girl." Horace being my dad's name.

One pub we went to, the landlord would give me a package wrapped up in newspaper and told me not to open it until I got home. We would smile at each other with a nod and

I would then thank him very quietly.

The parcel contained Cats Muck. Well, that's what we were told to call it. To be honest it did look like a blob of dried cats poo, but it was really raw chocolate from the Cadbury factory at Frampton-on-Severn and it was our special treat. It was very hard. Mum would break it with the flat iron and we were allowed a small piece every now and again. We were never quite sure if we would ever have any more so we made it last a long time.

When I was home from school on holiday Dad would use these days to have me help him in the mill. The task was usually to clean out the big vats. They stood about fifteen foot high and had an opening on the top of about two foot, six inches square. A ladder was dropped down inside and a ladder on the outside. Dad would work inside the vat, getting out all the gungy mess from the bottom of the vat, carrying it up the ladder and putting the bucket on the platform at the top. My job was to empty the buckets as he brought them up. They were too heavy for me to take down my ladder but I would pour half into a small bucket and go up and down the ladder that way, always checking on Dad to make sure the fumes and gases inside the vat hadn't overcome him. He always had a long piece of pipe down there with him so he could draw fresh air from the outside. Me and my dad made a great team.

Another lovely day I always looked

forward to was the cooper coming to mend all of the barrels. I made sure I kept him supplied with wood for his fire and made sure his cider supply never ran out. I loved watching him at work.

My dad and Ernie (Jennifer's Father)

13. CHRISTMAS

Childhood Christmases were really very special and as children it was something we looked forward to for weeks ahead. Mum made the Christmas cake and Christmas pudding. We all had to wish while stirring the mixture. Dad and I would make trips into the woods to find a Christmas tree, some holly with berries and mistletoe. We would have walnuts and hazelnuts and chestnuts which had been collected before the squirrels had taken them all. Pears and apples came out of the cold store, which, in our case, was under the stairs, and not to forget the homemade wine. Paper chains were made and decorations for the tree came out of hiding. A few new ones were always made. There was also the Sunday School Christmas party to look forward to and that night finally came when you could hang one of Dad's socks on the bottom of the bed, hoping it would be full in the morning. And it always was. There were nuts in the toe, an orange in the heel, sweets and a special present. One year I had a Timex watch and another year I had a very nice scarf. Oh, Christmas was such a joyous time. I remember my baby brother, Roger, had a teddy bear that actually growled. I loved it and kept it for years. I gave it back to my brother on his fiftieth birthday.

The highlight of Christmas morning was my dad's boss coming to visit us. He always gave us kids a tin of toffees to share between us. It was always a very pretty tin and Mum would keep each tin to store things in when it was empty. I remember there was once a lovely one with a robin on it.

Oh what beautiful, wonderful days. The years passed by so quickly with a mixture of cider making, fruit picking, bird nesting, exploring the woods, looking after my baby brother, school, Sunday School and helping my dad in the garden. We grew all of our own veg. The garden was my dad's pride and joy. We did really live off it all the year round. Like I said before, my dad was a really good provider and we ate well and my mum was a wonderful cook and I always helped her with the jam making and bottling fruit.

MARRIED LIFE

14. SOUL MATES

I was still at school when I met my husband, Dal. My best friend at school was Pat Bennett. She lived in Mitcheldean. We walked to her house for lunch each day. I remember us watching Pebble Mill so that would have been about 1957. How many of you remember that? Well, her brother, Pete, was best friends with someone called Dal Weaver and when walking back to school up Abenhall pitch we would meet Dal as he was going home for his lunch. He had a motorbike and worked on the farm next to the school. He and Pat were always nattering about something.

The day after my fifteenth birthday I went to school and Pat wasn't there so at lunch time I walked to her house to find out why. I think she said she had a cold or something. Anyway, I walked back to school on my own. Dal came down on his motorbike, stopped and asked where I had been yesterday as I hadn't been at school. I told him that I had been to the dentist and wasn't very happy about it because it was my birthday. "Oh," he said, "that wasn't very nice, was it?"

The next time we met he asked if I would like a ride on his motorbike. Me, the biggest tomboy that ever walked, riding on a motorbike. As if I'd ever pass up such a chance! It was arranged for Saturday evening because he had to work all day Saturday. (Well, men did in those days). I told my mum and she said I would need a pair of trousers. "You can't be going on a motorbike in a dress," she'd said so by Saturday I was the proud owner of a pair of trousers.

We started going out just before Christmas. We used to go to the pictures sometimes but by the time Dal had rode to my house on his motorbike he was far too cold to go anywhere until it was time for him to go home, so Mum allowed me to light the fire in the front room and we listened to the radio.

He became my boyfriend well and truly and there was no other boy for me. He probably wasn't quite as smitten as me but he was mine and he soon got used to the idea. He was twenty-one and had never had a girlfriend before, only mates, and it came as a bit of a shock.

Every other Sunday he had to do the milking and I would go and do the afternoon milking with him. The boss's wife would come out with tea and cake, homemade of course. I enjoyed my Sundays with the cows.

That following year I was working and trying to save money to get married. Dal had never saved a penny and it was an uphill struggle to get him to part with a few shillings to put in the TSB but I persevered. He had his own bank book and when he realised that the money soon mounted up he gradually gave me more to put in the bank.

Dad heard of some land that had come up

for sale. It was a four acre orchard of Blaisden plums. He said it would be a good investment so we went to see Mr. Bowkett, the man who was selling it. We bought it and we spent all the spare time we had over there, tidying and repairing the hedgerows and doing whatever else needed attention. We had a shed in the quarry hole and if it rained we could work in there. So, we kept ourselves busy with no need to go out and spend money (and we needed our money to enable us to get married). That coming year we had a marvellous crop of plums. Dad had been right. We got our money back in the first year.

I was working in a laundry office and we had a small shop at the front of the office. If a customer came in, a bell would ring and I would go and serve them. I made friends with nurse Morgan who came in once a week with her laundry. I also served her husband, Bill, when he brought his dirty overalls in. He worked at the wagon works and we did a special overall wash for them. Anyway, nurse Morgan was telling me how she had this bungalow on the side of the canal that she and Bill never used and were going to sell it. It was fully furnished and had a generator for electric. You couldn't live there full time but you could use it for weekends or holidays. Was it of any interest to me and my boyfriend? Her and Bill wanted £250 for it. I said we would be very interested and I would let her know after the weekend.

We had enough money saved to buy it. We thought that we might be able to get planning permission to put it in on our orchard as we'd already been thinking of building where the shed stood in the quarry hole in the centre of the land. Of course we said yes and we were now the proud owners of Webber's Post.

We started putting our plans into action and applied for planning permission. In the meantime we were enjoying Sundays on the canal in our little but perfect home. The generator worked a treat, much to the delight of that man of mine. We lit the fire and had enough food for the day. We still only had a motorbike so I carried most things in a rucksack on my back. Dal would have a bag on the tank between his legs.

That year we had another good crop of plums and we had enough money to put our plans in action just as soon as we got planning permission but, guess what, the buggers turned us down. They said the roads weren't good enough for a district nurse and doctor to drive down but we would have done the road up obviously.

In the meantime we heard of three building plots coming up for sale at May Hill. We went after one and bought the large top one for £500. That was all of our money gone. We applied to move our wooden bungalow there. They would only allow it if we bricked around it, so we had to agree. More expense. We already had the expense of the foundation because the ground was on such a slope the foundation on the bottom end was eight feet deep tapering off to nothing towards the entrance from the road but we had an acre plot next to my beloved brook that ran to Deep Filling and we had woods on both sides and a lovely outlook.

In the spring of 1961 we started building. We had to take up a £1000 mortgage with the Co-op. The date was set for the wedding, 2nd September that year. We just hoped the building was finished by then. We decided to call our cottage DALAPAM.

I made my own wedding dress of satin and lace. The two bridesmaids were Dal's nieces and his nephew was pageboy. Gordon Hyett, our friend, made the three tier wedding cake and did the reception at May Hill Hall. I was eighteen years old when we married at Huntley Church. The guests passed DALAPAM on their way to the reception so it was open for everyone to see and it was finished in good time. We honeymooned on the Isle of Man because it was when the finale of the TT racing was on. I had wanted to go to Jersey and was promised we would go to Jersey the following year, but by June the following year Martin was born, so we never got there and guess what, in fifty years of married life we never got to Jersey and I still haven't been to this day but it is on my list of things I must try to do.

Me and Dal on our wedding day

15. BECOMING MUM

Married life was good and in no time at all I was leaving work and getting ready to have our much wanted baby. I always knew I was expecting a boy and I named him Mark. Everything I knitted was trimmed with blue so it had to be a boy. The day he was born I changed my mind about the name, changing it to Martin. He was my pride and joy. Mum and Dad came to see us at the weekend and Mum asked what had made me change his name. I really couldn't explain it but Martin it was going to be. She looked at me and said to me that her mother's maiden name was Martin, Fanny Martin. I can honestly say I did not know that. Of course, Mum was pleased but to this day I have no idea why I changed it.

God works in mysterious ways, as my mum would say.

I soon got into a routine. Having a baby really suited me. Most days I would go and visit Mum. It was mainly downhill except for the last hill up to Hill View (my childhood family home). We always had so much to talk about.

The return journey home was up hill all the way and I really had to get my back into pushing that pram, but it kept me fit.

On my 21st birthday I went into hospital to have my second child, but didn't have her until two days later, on my mother-in-laws birthday, so that made her very pleased and I loved Dal's Mum. We now had a beautiful baby girl called Belinda. It was the terrible winter of 1963 and me and my two babies were house bound for weeks.

I must tell you another extraordinary story of when our youngest daughter was born. We, of course, had to choose a name for her. I only gave our children one name because Dal had two given names and two nick names and

I always had to think what people called him before referring to him. Christmas cards were a nightmare.

His mother and sister called him George, his ex-school teacher, who we lived next door to, called him Raymond, my family and I called him Dal, and all his work mates called him Danny, so I had to be really careful when signing cards. Our children were only having one name and one name only.

Louisa was the name chosen for our second daughter and life fell into a new pattern with a new baby. I hadn't had one for four years so it was quite a new experience with nappies and all that went with a baby in the house. Anyway, I reckon Louisa was about a month old. I was visiting my mum while the other children were at school when all of sudden she told me that she hadn't put Louisa's birthday in the birthday book. Mum had her mother's birthday book which had been given to her on her mother's 21st birthday. On the inside page it says "To my dear Fanny, on her 21st birthday with love from sister Bessie." Well, Mum got the book out of the drawer, came to the table and sat down and started to turn the pages. She turned to me and asked what date Louisa was born. I told her the 14th of June and she turned to the 14th June and there, written on the page was aunt Louisa, born 1843. What a coincidence. We could not believe it. I have Mum's birthday book now and it is a most treasured possession.

Family photo 1990

16. A LOVING HOME

A house very close to ours came up for sale, called The Arches. It was just what we wanted. It had enough land for us to be able to keep some animals and more bedrooms for all six children that I had planned to have. We put our place on the market and were finally selling it to a lovely couple, Tim and Dorothy. They were getting married and our house was just what they were looking for. (By the way, they are still there to this day, fifty-two years later). We went round to the people who owned The Arches to tell them that we had sold our place and were now ready to buy but that day they had just signed to sell it to someone else. We were devastated. It was not going to be easy finding another place with land on it. Tim and Dorothy were desperate for us not to pull out so we ended up buying a three-bedroom semi-detached at Churcham just to see us over while we looked for another property. Five years later and two more children (Louisa and Nicholas) we found The Old Mill at Moreton Valence, with enough land for some animals (four acres) and a lovely stream, the Arle Brook, that ran the boundary of the land and through the garden with two waterfalls and a weir.

It was a lovely old house. The deeds went back four-hundred years. Our solicitor was very interested to find out more about it. He told us it went back to Victorian times and the last thing to be made in the mill was pins.

We had a lot of repairs to do, especially on the third floor. It had been taken over by birds. We got two bedrooms repaired and moved the three eldest children up there. The kitchen and bathroom on the ground floor were in a lean-to and beyond repair so it had to be demolished so we made a make-do kitchen on the first floor, next to the bathroom and the one and only toilet. I don't remember it being a bad time. It had to be done and I accepted it as a challenge.

One of the out buildings was full of oak floor blocks that had been there for years. We found out from the woman we bought the house from that her husband worked for the GPO and the blocks were originally taken out of the offices when they were demolished so they were very old indeed. The previous owners had laid some of them in the sitting room and, sanded up, they looked gorgeous. I set to, sorting the blocks out. The shed was an old stone tiled building and quite damp and dark so I brought the blocks out in a wheelbarrow into the daylight. It had been a long time since they had seen the light of day. A lot of them were going rotten but they would burn well on the Rayburn so they went off to the wood shed. The sorting continued whenever I had a spare half hour. I neatly packed the blocks into boxes and all the off-cuts went into hessian sacks. The plan was for them to be laid in the dining room if we had enough.

The time came to lay the blocks. We didn't really know what we were doing but we had the sitting room floor to help us. We had been told to set them in a film of tar to even them up and make them secure. We just went for it, Dal kneeling and laying the blocks and me keeping the supplies coming. We decided to do a block edging, three deep, laying the blocks like brickwork and then a herring bone design in the centre. We were told not to worry about the gaps as we would fill them in at the very end.

We spent all of our spare time on that floor not knowing whether we had enough blocks or not. I just kept bringing the boxes in and watching the stack of boxes going down. We had finally finished. We filled all of the cracks in with the off cuts that I had saved. If we didn't have a perfect fit we cut one to size. We were now experts at laying block flooring and guess what, I reckon we had enough blocks over to do the hallway too!

We hired a sanding machine and began sanding our hopeful master piece. It came up like brand new and it was glorious, a real work of art. What a clever pair of buggers we were. We did the hall that joined the sitting room and dining room together. The hall was done in brickwork design and still we had some blocks left over. I still wonder how old the blocks really are. In a couple of years we had the house all repaired; new kitchen, new shower room on the ground floor and new bathroom on the first floor and washroom on the top floor. We had almost an acre of vegetable garden which kept me busy most of my spare time and a really large poly-tunnel that I could always work in when it was raining so we were producing more than enough fruit and veg. for our own needs. Living on the A38 was an advantage because when I had a bumper crop of beans, tomatoes, eggs and what-not, I put a sign up on the road and everything soon went. Dal used to get up early and dig me rows of new planting space that became available from the finished crops. I would then replant it and so it went on. In the evening, I would water it all with buckets of fresh water from the stream or water butts. There's nothing like natural water to make things grow.

The children had a large, above-the-ground swimming pool, so on a warm summer's evening, when the kids were all in bed and I had tidied up the garden and done all the watering, I would strip off and have a swim.

Two or three times a week Dal would drive for our neighbour, collecting cattle for market and not coming home until early in the morning. He'd grab a couple of hours sleep and then be back to his regular job. It was the only way of earning some extra money.

17. FOSTERING

I was never going to have our six children as I had been strongly advised not to have any more after my last baby, so I got to thinking about fostering and so that was the start of another adventure in our lives. We had to make sure our own children were happy about it. The girls couldn't wait and were really excited. Nick just went along with anything. He would have a new playmate. Martin was worried he might have to share his bedroom. It was carefully discussed with our social worker and we decided it would be nice to have children of the same age as ours and always younger than Martin who was then ten years old. The children we had were mainly short term, that way I would not get too attached to them. Your allowance for the children was not a great amount but there's not a lot of difference between catering for four or eight children. You were given a monthly clothes allowance and pocket money for each child, according to their age. I told the social worker there was no way I could give them pocket money, as our own children didn't have it and I felt it would cause problems between them. The social worker looked at me very hard and said, "Well, you can't keep it!" I said, "Of course not".

After some thought it was decided that I would open up a TSB account and put the pocket money into that and they would take the book with them when they left. In the meantime they got paid for doing jobs around the house and garden, the same as our children did. Most of the foster children came out of children's homes and, according to how long they had been in care, determined how institutionalised they were and how many of the tricks they had picked up. A favourite one was that if you didn't like your trousers, for example, you would (accidently) rip them and the next morning you would get a new pair. Well, that didn't work in our home. If they ripped their trousers when staying with us, the torn trousers were repaired or patched.

We had a lovely wooden play house in the garden which was always a great hit with new children. I soon worked out that the most daunting thing for a new young child was coming to the dinner table, so whoever they had palled-up with I suggested they laid the table in the playhouse and have their meal out there. They soon settled in and it was very rewarding to see them happy and blooming and adjusting to their new way of life.

Saturday afternoon was the day we went to a jumble sale. The children would take their money earned during the week and buy maybe a book or toy or game. I would be busy buying them clothes as we got through quite a lot on the farm as someone was always falling over in the mud or getting wet through in the stream.

Finally, we all filed into the car with our treasures, all happy bunnies. My job when I got home was to put the washing machine on and wash all my new purchases, hopefully to be able to put them out on the washing line and view them from the kitchen window with great satisfaction. By the time they were ironed, and maybe the odd repair made, they looked like new.

We carried on fostering for about six years and then it was decided we would cut down. Gradually we stopped and fully intended to start up again when our own children had flown the nest.

18. EXTRA MEMBER OF OUR FAMILY

When we moved to The Old Mill in 1971 it was a really big adventure for the whole family. The house was so much bigger than anything we had been used to. It was very old with sheds everywhere and an old two storey stable with all the lovely horse dividers still intact. Everywhere was full of old junk because we had told the elderly lady who was moving out that we would get rid of the rubbish for her. One stone building was full of old TV sets. We came to the conclusion that someone at sometime had been into repairing TVs.

The old brick stable block was also cramped with junk and cobwebs hung everywhere. There was an old iron ladder that took you up to the floor above which was strewn with old papers and boxes. There was something very spooky about this place and I rarely went up there. I used to go into the bottom stable quite a bit, either tidying up or to put things in there, but every time I was in there, I always got the feeling I was not alone and would not hang around for too long. Time passed very quickly at our new home with so much that needed doing and four energetic children running about the place. Funny, unexplainable things kept happening, and over a period of time it felt like we had an invisible child about the place, who was playing tricks. In the end, we gave this invisible person a name and he or she was known to the whole family as Fred.

Anything that happened which could not be explained Fred got the blame. They were harmless things that would happen and we never ever got alarmed about it. Things like the TV changing channels or suddenly going quiet or loud. Doors opening and shutting while we were all sat quietly watching TV.

One of us would shout, "Stop it, Fred." He was becoming one of the family.

One of the strangest things that ever happened was when I had a young lad doing some painting around the house for me. I would set him to work, maybe up on the first floor landing, leaving him with a radio for company while I went off to do my rounds, checking cattle. I was now renting extra land for my Dexters so the rounds took a while. About two hours later I returned to a very anxious young lad saying, "Pam, someone's been here turning the radio to other stations and, when I came down the stairs to check no-one was here and when I went back up, it happened again!" "Oh," I said, "don't worry about that, it's only Fred playing around." "Who's Fred?" he asked. "Our ghost," I said, "but he don't do any harm." He looked at me probably thinking I had lost my marbles!

Later that day, as he was going home, we were stood talking in the sitting room and he flicked his hands through his hair and two wooden beads rolled across the carpet. I bent down and picked them up and asked where they came from. He said that they had fallen out of the ceiling. I remarked that they couldn't have as we renewed all that when we moved in. "It's Fred, he don't like you. He must have thrown them at you." I said to him. The poor young lad left thinking the woman's mad. I looked at the beads in the palm of my hand. They were really old. One was smaller than the other, very well worn and quite the nicest little beads I had ever seen made of wood. I carried them across to the television and carefully placed them in a silver cup on top of the TV. Later that night, I said to Dal "I've got something to show you" and I got out of my armchair and walked across to the telly, picked the cup up and to my disappointment there were no beads in it. I have never seen those beads since.

Fred had been part of our family for about twenty-five years. We didn't really discuss him outside the family because people wouldn't have believed us and would not really think what we were saying was really true.

The children were leaving home and Fred was more quiet than usual. One night, in the early hours of the morning, just as it was getting light, Dal woke up, sat up in bed and asked if I was alright. I woke up and put my hand out and felt him and asked what was wrong. He turned to me and said "I thought that was you sat on the bottom of the bed." I looked and couldn't see anyone. Dal was completely sure there was someone sat on the bed but they were smaller than me and dressed in a nightdress. So, our Fred turned out to be a little girl after all this time. That explained a lot of things that had happened over the years. Fred always seemed to be in the girls' bedrooms, moving things about. Also, one morning, my youngest daughter Louisa was late coming downstairs. I said she'd be late for the school bus and she said she knew that but Fred had been sitting on her bed, rocking backwards and forwards and she didn't like to disturb him. That made sense now, a little girl sucking her thumb and rocking.

My son Nick now has the stable block over The Old Mill that has been made into a barn conversion and he says Fred visits on rare occasions. One Christmas we had snow over night and in the morning Nick went for a walk down the garden. A blanket of snow lay all around, completely untouched, and there, suddenly, were some little footprints around the wood pile. They started and ended from nowhere. Later that morning he asked me how big I thought Fred's footprints would be. I said four to five inches. He told me his story and we nodded and smiled at each other.

19. PONIES

When our own girls were old enough, it didn't take much persuading on their part, to get us to agree to a pony or two. The first pony was Seamus, a black Welsh gelding. It didn't take long to discover that he was a little bugger and knew all the tricks to get the rider off. He had to go. We would be more careful in our choice of pony next time. Well, I heard of a lovely little pony that had been with the same family for a long time and their children needed something bigger, so we became the proud owners of Wombles, the sweetest little pony that ever lived.

Later, we were offered another pony called Rupert, again a real sweetie, until you went cross-country on him. He was so keen that you had virtually no brakes and steering was very difficult but the girls loved him. Horses and ponies became a way of life and to this very day the girls and granddaughters still ride almost every day. I rode for a while but as the horses got more competitive, they became too strong for me. The day I fell off twice was the day I decided my riding days were over.

Horses and horse talk play a large part in our lives. Martin works in a racing stables so we all have a lot in common. We have the "Migh Team" of horses and the "Migh Team" of Dexters, so plenty to keep us all on our toes!

SHOWING

20. GETTING INTO DEXTERS

I got into Dexters when my husband suggested I should keep some cows because they were good for the land after years of ponies and horses. He worked full-time so they would be my responsibility. I chose Dexters because they were small and more easy to manage and we only had four acres of land at that time. Dal couldn't get his head around Dexters and thought I should have what he called a proper breed. I stood my ground and insisted on Dexters. I soon found out it was easier said than done. In the 1970s Dexters were a rare breed and very hard to get hold of so I went to the local market to see if anything else took my fancy and then one Monday, Monday being market day, this tiny little baby Hereford heifer came in. Oh, she was so tiny and cute and definitely what no proper farmer would take home. She was in great need of TLC and lots of warmth as it was winter time. Eventually, she came though the auction ring and I started bidding.

She was mine. One old farmer turned to me and said, "You will need a bit of luck with that my dear." I quickly went and paid for her, ran and got my pick-up truck, piled loads of straw in the back and got her out of the pen with all the other calves in. It took a while to spot her as all the others were so much bigger than she was. She was found and the lovely market man carried her in his arms to my truck. I had a canopy on my pick-up so she was buried in straw and as snug as a bug in a rug. When I got home I made her a den out of straw bales with a roof which was an old wooden door. On the way home I had called in to the animal feed merchant for a bag of milk powder, which I remembered cost me more than the calf had. Oh, she must live or my little project would be a failure. I made up the milk powder, nice and warm. I knew she would be too young to drink so I put my fingers in the milk mixture and got her to suck my fingers time and time again. I did this until she was really getting a taste of the milk and eager for more then I lowered my fingers into the milk. She was now really sucking my fingers and drinking the milk. We were away and with all the milk almost gone I was away to the house for a cup of tea. I gave her a really long name because she was so small, Willamena. She was a little gem with big eyes and white face. I was still looking for a Dexter without much joy but, never mind, I had Willamena. I went to the Royal Show at Stoneleigh and I knew there would be Dexters there so at least I could get to talk with breeders. Well, my luck was in and I talked to a lady who had a herd of Dexters that she milked and sold off the heifers as they were born. The only trouble was, she had a waiting list, but at least I was now on the list. All I had to do was wait for the phone call.

The call came about five months later, just before Christmas. She had been on her mother for five days and was ready for collection. At that time the weather was bad and we had to go to Tavistock to pick her up.

We had a mate who went that way every

week with a large artic. cattle lorry but that would have been too stressful for her, so a plan was worked out. We would load our pick-up onto the lorry that was going down past Tavistock empty. He would drop us off in a lay-by and we would bring her home in our pick-up.

It all sounded so simple. We would drive up the tail board just like that. Ha! Well, eventually, with the help of a ramp and a couple of planks we were on and on our way. A lovely journey sharing all the gossip and news on the way and before too long we were very close to Tavistock and dropping off time. We found a lay-by, the tailboard came down and our mate and Dal announced that I had to reverse the pick-up down while he and Dal held the tailboard up to meet the step that was about nine inches up to the floor of the container. The two men held the tailboard up, shouting for me to reverse. As soon as the weight of the pick-up hit the tailboard the two strong men, so they thought, couldn't hold the weight and, bang, down went the tailboard with me and the pick-up coming down and off at great speed. With no-one hurt and exhaust pipe still intact, we were on our way.

Deal done, I was now the proud owner of a Dexter heifer, Larush the 4th of Knotting. This was her pedigree name. She was lovely. Two years later she produced for me a beautiful little bull calf which I called Willi-do-it because I thought, one day, he might! I showed Willi the following year and soon found he wasn't quite as good as I thought he was, but I had got the bug for showing. Everyone was so friendly and I met Eileen who was as keen as me and we became the best of friends. Over the following winter I scoured the country looking for some nice show quality heifers and managed to get three - Jollity, Mamba and Juniper.

Me with Jaymark Gypsy Jollity

Me with Migh Rufus

Gosh, didn't we have some fun. I had an old Bedford lorry with a leaking radiator which I had to top up every hundred miles. Eileen and her boyfriend, Wally, followed with their caravan and we travelled miles, showing our beloved animals.

Me with Gloucester Cow

21. THE SHOW LIFE

Showing cattle is a wonderful way of life. It is very hard work but you are surrounded by animals and people who love looking after them.

Showing any animal is something to take very seriously. You and your animals are shown to the public and you have to be very professional in your attitude. You and your animals must always be clean and smart and you must always respect the judge, as he or she is master of the day and at the end of judging, it's nice that we, as exhibitors, feel that the judge got it right. I was a judge for a great number of years and I would like to think I got it right. When I first started judging, I used to tell myself that I was there to choose the best animal to take home for myself, so I would check them all for correctness, shape, condition and quietness. If they wouldn't stand still, how could I judge them?

Me judging at Royal Cornwall Show

At the end of judging my champion was the animal I would like most to take home to join my herd. It would be my type of animal. It may not be everyone's choice but it was mine and that's the one I wanted. Of course, the owner would never part with it!

One-day shows are really hard work. Your day would start at about 4:30am, loading the animals (you had hopefully loaded everything else the night before) and travelling miles to the show. There'd hopefully be no queue to get in and, of course, you'd pray for a fine, dry day as there's nothing worse than being out in the rain all day. You'd then wash the cattle, bed them down on nice clean golden straw, give them a nice feed of hay and water, hoping they wouldn't tip the water bucket over the minute you turned your back. You'd then go and collect your numbers and hand in your passports.

Every animal has a passport. You have to fill it in and register that it left your farm. The show has to book it in. They also have to book it off for you to leave and then when you get home you have to book it back onto your farm. In what we refer to as the good old days we had none of this rigmarole. We could go and do whatever we liked and do two or three shows without even going home. Now the paperwork and rules and regulations make it impossible. I have two isolation units on the farm so that does help with my movements but the paperwork is still terrible.

When the shows are three or four days long, it is like going on holiday and taking your animals along. We are all there to work hard and have some fun in the evenings when the visitors have gone home. It's either a get-together on the cattle lines or a party in someone's lorry. We always had Chris with us, sometimes showing his own Dexters or helping me and Eileen with ours. After partying we would always go and check the animals. One night Eileen and Chris were busy watering and bedding down as an elderly couple came along. We talked about the state of farming. They had a farm which they were about to give up as none of their children wanted to take it over. Chris, a lovely young lad about twenty years old, and Eileen, came walking towards us, their work all finished. The woman said to me, "Well, you won't have our problems, your children are more than keen." I said, and I don't know what made me say it, "Oh, they are nothing to do with me. They're just hangers on." Eileen looked at me with such a sad face and quietly said, "Oh Mum, why do you say such awful things?" to which Chris added, "just because we have different fathers."

The women looked at me in disgust, grabbed her husband's arm and they both walked off down the shed at speed. The three of us looked at one another and burst out laughing. I couldn't help laughing and I couldn't believe what had just been said. We must have had too much to drink that night. It was just out of the blue and why it was said or where it came from is still a mystery.

Showing in those early days was wonderful. We were all so friendly. Everyone helped each other and at the local one-day shows we all pooled our food and had a picnic.

Get together at Monmouth Show

The Welsh shows were the best. We met some wonderful characters. We used to go to

Swansea Show and the wonderful old gentleman in charge of the cattle would do a running commentary while we were in the grand parade. He would say to everyone in his lovely Welsh accent, "and now we have Mrs. Weaver with her lovely Dexters, all the way from Gloucester, England."

Eileen would relay this to everyone on our return home and she was really good because she was able to do the Welsh accent really well. Oh, what happy times we had.

Animals done. Now it's my turn thanks to Eileen

At the height of my showing Eileen and I did forty shows a year, talked to thousands of people, have seen show people come and go and we are still there enjoying every minute of it.

Hot air ballooning, aerial view of the Three Counties Showground

22. HAIR-CUT DAY AT EGHAM SHOW

Every year, towards the end of the show season, I would go to Egham show. It was one of my favourite shows. I don't know why but I have got quite a few fond memories of Egham. It was a two-day show, so you would travel there on the Friday, ready for judging on the Saturday morning. Usually it was a show that Eileen would not want to miss but I remember there was one year when she could not manage to come with me so I got my friend Pam Smith to agree to come. I had known Pam for many years from the children's Pony Club & Riding Club days so I knew she was used to handling horses. There was not a lot of difference, or so I thought, but there was, as Pam was keen to tell me, "They have runny, messy toilet habits." She did have a point. Horse poo is quite firm where as a cow is quite a different story. I tried to reassure her that my cattle were kept in the barn between shows and were quite firm. Problem solved! I then said we would be going the night before and sleeping in the lorry.

"Oh no," she said, "I can't sleep rough." and she dug her heels in on that one, so we were going to travel up early in the morning, at some unearthly hour.

The traffic must have been bad or maybe I misjudged the timing of the journey because we were late arriving and only got there about fifteen minutes before judging. The lovely stewards helped me to unload the animals and I asked Pam to get a bucket and find some water so we could wash the muck off their bums. I had them tied up at the washing bay and told Pam to grab a brush and wash off the muck. The next thing I knew she was gone so I got on with it and was nearly finished when Pam came back, busily putting on a pair of yellow rubber gloves. I just froze to the spot, not knowing whether to laugh, cry or just die! Somehow, I gathered myself together and we got into the ring and I am sure we managed to take the Championship. Needless to say, Pam never came showing with me again. We are still the best of friends and still have a good laugh about her one and only day showing cattle. Bless her!

Also, at Egham show, it became an annual hair cutting day, as one of our fellow exhibitors was a hairdresser. So, after judging we would all queue up to have our hair cut by the lovely Mary.

Another time, yet again at Egham, I

remember, and I don't actually know why, but Dal had come with me. It was always nice to have him with us because he was always so good at getting the cows' udders just right for the show ring. There is a real art to getting it just right and because he had hand-milked all his life he was so good at it.

The first thing we do after judging is let the calves suckle their mothers but you must not let them have too much all at once so when the calf has had enough we put it back in the pen and then milk off some more milk to ease the udder and make the cow more comfortable. Dal was busy milking when a woman stopped with her young son. She was telling him this was where his milk came from. Her youngster was not interested and Dal carried on milking, letting the milk go into the straw as there was no point saving it. The mother was still determined for her son to understand. He was about to do a runner so she grabbed his arm and said in a very loud voice, "Do you now understand where your milk comes from?" "No," he said, "how do they get it up from the floor?" Needless to say we all burst out laughing and we had a bit of explaining to do. My beloved Dexters have given me so many wonderful memories.

Back in the eighties when I first started showing my lovely little cows and bulls, things were much different in those days and I must say much better and far more fun. We would all help each other. It was a time with good honest country people who solely worked for the welfare of their animals. We were all friends, with some really lovely old characters amongst them. I loved them all for their knowledge and helpfulness.

One evening, when all of the work was done I got a bucket of hot water from the dairy as it was time to think about bed. I was saying goodnight to everyone and one of them ask me what the bucket of hot water was for. I said I was going to have a bath in the bucket. They laughed and asked if I needed some help. I said that I didn't as I had it off to a fine art. I said that I would start at the top and finish at the bottom. I bid them all good night and trundled back to my lorry with my bucket of precious hot water. I knew I would feel so nice after a wash and hopefully sleep well. Next morning, I was up bright and early and eager to see my cows. As

I entered the cattle shed and walked towards my cattle, a cheer went up and I noticed my lovely mates had made me a shower. They had used bales of straw, pitch forks and a piece of tarpaulin and made a sign saying 'Mrs Weaver's Shower' and Jim Howie was ready with the hose pipe. Such lovely people. Sadly, Jim is no longer with us.

Me with the lovely Jim Howie

23. CHESHIRE SHOW

We were at Cheshire Show when my husband, Dal, got an unexpected shock that caused much hilarity.

In preparation for a show, cattle have to be washed, dried, brushed, and titivated and then, just before they go into the ring, they have their hooves and horns (if they have them) oiled and any missed bits of dirt removed. Just before that though, the handlers have to tidy themselves up, for they also have to look smart in the show ring. Due to the messy nature of cow shampooing this usually means a change of clothes or, at the very least, a change of shirt and trousers. Dal had just put on a brand new fresh-out-of-the-packet, white shirt when he spotted a speck of dirt on our potential champion's udder so he bent down to clean it away and at that exact moment Polly the cow lifted her tail and coughed, emitting a stream of smelly brown poo. The unfortunate Dal was right in the firing line and a stinking stain spread all down the front of his brand new shirt. To make matters worse, as he stood up, the smelly brown mess slowly trickled into the chest pocket of the once pristine shirt.

Although this happened a long time ago, I reckon some of the exhibitors who were there at the time are still laughing to this day!

Let it be a warning to you all when visiting an agricultural show never to be behind a cow when she lifts her tail, especially if she coughs at the same time. I have seen many such accidents in my time and I still can't help laughing!!

24. HOLY COW

Another happy meeting occurred at the Three Counties Show when a group of vicars visited the cattle sheds. The three counties are Herefordshire, Worcestershire and Gloucestershire. Each year, in turn, one of those counties sends a group of clergymen and women to the show to represent the church. This particular year they came from the diocese of Hereford. When they introduced themselves we found out that each one of them had a farming background.

The Three Counties show has a magnificent grand parade of animals, every day of the show, held in the main arena. The show committee try to get as many animals as

possible into the arena and encourage all the
exhibitors to get their entire show teams out
on parade. Naturally, this is limited by the
number of competent handlers available.

Never one to miss an opportunity, I asked
the reverend gentlemen if they'd each like to
lead one of my Dexters in the grand parade
and they all eagerly agreed. Fully decked out in
smart, white stockman's coats and complete
with their dog collars we managed to get all
our cattle out to the parade.

The major prizes are presented in the
arena during the grand parade and on this
occasion the prize-giving was being conducted
by a member of the Royal Family. No names,
to protect the innocent, but it was a princess.
Following the handing out of the various
trophies this charming lady walked among the
animals and seeing our vicars, she made her
way over. She admired the cattle then asked,
"May I ask why you're wearing a dog collar?"
to which one of our vicars replied, "Well, it's
because I'm a vicar Ma'am" to which our
slightly embarrassed princess turned to her
husband and said, "Oh, how silly of me" but,
to be fair, our team of vicars are the only

clergymen we have ever seen leading cattle on grand parade so it was unusual, to say the least, so the princess' question wasn't so silly after all.

After the parade everyone wanted to know what had been said to the vicar and he was pleased to report on the question asked but added that, when he gave his reply, it had crossed his mind to say "Well, it's because I'm a gynaecologist Ma'am," but he held his tongue!

These lovely vicars still visit us at the show when it's the turn of the diocese of Hereford to send their church representatives and we enjoy catching up with them.

Some thirty years on I think they're still the only clergymen to have led cattle on grand parade.

25. COW POWER

We speak to lots of people at the shows. Some people are interested in buying Dexters, some are just curious about the breed and some just wanted to ask general questions about cows. Often, we'd get groups of school children in the cattle sheds with their teachers and they'd ask lots of questions. One day, at the Three Counties Show, a group of young children from a local special needs school visited the cattle sheds and were eager to see the animals. However, one little lad seemed much quieter and more timid than the rest so Eileen asked him if he would like to stroke the cows and, after asking the teacher if it was okay, held out her hand to him. He put his little hand in hers and she showed him our new Mum, Jollity and her calf and our bull, Eric. She lifted him up so he could feel their horns and stroke their backs. This little chap said nothing but was clearly enjoying his close-up-and-personal time with the animals. Eileen explained that Jollity was the mummy and Eric was the daddy and that the calf was their baby and the youngster enjoyed more time stroking them.

The teacher said it was time to leave so the little boy was handed back but, just before leaving, he turned to his teacher and said "Daddy cow, mummy cow, baby cow, horns". The teacher thanked us and off they went.

Sometime, later in the day, the teacher came back to see us to tell us that the little boy we'd talked to was extremely disturbed as a result of his dreadful background. She said that he could speak but chose not to as a reaction to his upbringing and the few words he'd spoken after stroking the cows (and apparently he'd said a little more as he left) were more words than he normally spoke in a week. This lovely teacher thanked us for the time we'd spent with him.

Eileen calls this Cow Power. She reckons you don't need to swim with dolphins, you can get the same sense of ease by being with cows for a while and you don't have to get wet either!

26. DEXTERS

Dexter cattle have been part of my life for over forty years. During that time they have brought me in contact with some lovely people.

The winning pair, 1998

Dexters originally came from Ireland and were a rare breed when I first started showing them. Irish people would say that they had never seen them in Ireland. Now the Irish farmers are very interested in them and we export hundreds of cattle to Ireland. They are not a rare breed anymore and haven't been for a number of years now.

Herd presentation at East of England Show

The Irish membership is growing year after year and to think they first came here one hundred and twenty years ago from Ireland, died out and are now making a complete come back. I think all my hours spent talking to would-be owners over the years have paid off.

When I first got my Dexters my husband wasn't all that keen on the breed. I had chosen them so they were referred to as, "the wife's cattle."

When I joined the Dexter Cattle Society I had to register a prefix so rather than saying "my" I thought of another way of spelling "my" as in "migh" and so it became "Migh Herd of Dexter Cattle."

Me and Eileen in our herd sweaters

As well as my cows (about thirty in the herd) I run six bulls which go out on hire to Dexter breeders all over the country, which is something I have been doing for many years now.

Trophies won in 1998

I am pleased I kept it going because it's a lovely way of keeping in touch with breeders and seeing their stock. You can AI (artificially inseminate) cows but it's not as good as running them with a bull. Most Dexter breeders only run a few cows and it doesn't justify buying a bull, and once the bull has served the cows, and they are all in calf, he is looking for new pastures green. With bulling cow and heifers it takes good fencing to keep a bull in, especially when he can smell love in the air down wind. My bulls have a good life, moving from one breeder to another every two or three months. They are very contented and don't get frustrated and they're never hard to load because they soon learn it is time to go to new pastures green and bull heaven.

Migh Eric at Frome Show, 1990

FILMING

27. HOW MY FILM LIFE STARTED

I was at Cheshire Show in 1989 when I was approached and asked about the possibility of doing a film with my cattle. They were looking for cows with horns. I agreed without even knowing what film it was. We were due to start in September, which was after the show season, so that was fine by me. The next conversation we had, I was asked if I had any goats and sheep with horns. Yes, I did. Then I was asked about geese and chickens. Again, yes, I said. It was then that I asked what sort of film were we doing and was told it was called Robin Hood: Prince of Thieves, and was told it was American. I asked if there was anyone famous in it and was told Kevin Costner. "Kevin who?" I asked, having never heard of him. He repeated himself but the name meant nothing to me. My friends kept on asking who was in this film I was doing. I told them Kevin somebody or other and so it went on.

The day arrived to start filming. My husband took the day off work and came with me along with a young friend of mine. We got dressed up as peasants so that we could always be with the animals. It was fascinating how everyone worked together.

Come lunch time we had so much to talk about. We were sat on the tailboard of our lorry, just down the track, away from the actual film set and I asked if anyone had seen Robin Hood but none of us had. All we had seen were forest men and women dressed like peasants. Then up the track came a lone figure looking very dashing in suede trousers and all the trimmings. All of sudden he was opposite me and I said, "Excuse me, are you Robin Hood?" and this big beaming smile came across his face and said, "I guess so." "So you must be Kevin Cog.....Cog...Cog" (I couldn't pronounce his name). He asked who I was and me, wishing the ground would open up and bury me, I said, "Oh, I'm no one, just Pam. I just look after the animals." He was still smiling and asked if we were having a good day. We carried on filming. It was such a magical day. The next time I saw Kevin he said, "Hi Pam, how's the animals?"

The next location was Alnwick Castle and so it went on for five months with me and Kevin becoming the best of friends. He loved the animals and would always spend his free time with them. He is one of the nicest people I have ever met.

One of the animals that soon became a firm favourite was Fred the Ram. He was a Jacob, with four big horns. He would roam the film set and all the extras would feed him tit bits they had kept by from lunchtime.

Fred the Ram

Next in line was Gertie the Goat. She was the one that stood out from all the rest.

Gertie the Goat

Through all my filming career I have always tried to get the shot that the director is seeking by using no cruelty. When you are working on a set you can have hundreds of eyes watching your every move, all ready to pounce if you put a foot wrong, so you handle your animals with extreme care and gentleness or you would be out of business straight away. I was working late one night with Fred the Ram and Kevin was perfecting the scene of Robin Hood jumping through a window and landing by Fred, close to the altar, with me just out of shot trying to keep Fred calm. We were never quite sure where Kev would land and the three of us would land in a heap. Each time the glass had to be replaced. It was sugar glass, so not harmful. Well, someone noticed Fred had runny eyes. I said it was due to the dust and that I had some eye cream and would treat it before he went to bed. A while later, it was thought we should call the vet so, at about 9:30pm, the vet was called. He arrived and filming stopped for Fred to be examined. The vet said that a bit of eye cream would put Fred right. He said that it was probably the dust. I said that I'd told them that and apologised for calling him out so late and he said that it was fine and that he had better come back and check him tomorrow, "What time is lunch?" and we all laughed. I made sure that production paid that bill and I had a fresh supply of eye cream!

Kevin with Fred the Ram

One day, while on set, I was approached by production who told me that I had to think of a name to call my animal company as I was now part of their production team and had to do my own invoicing and they needed to print me some letter headings. Things were moving a little fast for this country bumpkin. I said, "I'm Pam Weaver," to which I was told I could do better than that. "Well," I said, "everyone thinks the animals are almost human" and from that moment on my little enterprise was known as Almost Human

Animals.

The filming went on with me moving from one location to another and never going home as, although we had every Saturday and Sunday off, it was too much like hard work to move all the animals and too stressful for them, so my husband would visit me wherever I was and bring me clean clothes and the post, and take my dirty washing back home. The caterers would always leave me enough food for the weekend as I was usually miles from anywhere. I slept in the luton of my lorry and had a small gas stove to cook on. We then moved to Shepperton Studios for the last six to eight weeks of filming so I had a caravan and the back lot of the studios were converted into stables for the animals. By now it was November and getting colder. We were aiming to finish by Christmas but it never happened and we were all back at the beginning of January to try and finish it all in one week.

My husband came with me along with just the bare essential animals, mainly Fred the Ram. Everyone was talking about the wrap party. Something I had never heard of before but soon found out about. I found out that they always have one at the end of making a film. It was going to be at the BAFTA and everyone said that I must go. It was going to be held after our last filming day. I told my husband about it and that I should go but he was not in a very good mood. He had a bad cold (man flu) and said he couldn't understand me. I had been away from home for five months and I still wasn't satisfied. He said, "For goodness sake, come home." He did have a point and, in any case, I didn't really have anything to wear.

On the last day of filming we were all hanging around waiting for the final wrap to be announced and when it came everyone cheered and a make-up girl, who was sitting by me and Fred, jumped up and made her way towards Kevin as he came from the set, and had a kiss from him. I shouted over, "Hey Kev, can I have one of those?" and he said, "Get yourself in here, Pam." and I had the biggest smacker on the lips. I grabbed Fred and ran up the corridors, licking the grit from around my mouth that Kevin had left there because the scene that he had been doing was sword fighting with the sheriff and every time he hit the stone pillar where explosives had been planted, grit would fly onto his face which was covered in artificial sweat.

I got to the caravan, flung the door open and said to my beloved husband, "That's it, a final wrap, we can go home." He said, "What about this bloody party?" and I replied, "Oh, it don't matter about that. I've had such a smacker off Kev and I'm ready to go home." So the next morning we packed up the lorry with all the animals, hitched up the caravan and said goodbye to my incredibly tempting way of life with no wrap party.

When I was filming with Kev Costner (and I knew actually who he was now) life got into some sort of pattern and I was enjoying every minute of it. Every Friday evening Kev would fly back to L.A. on Concord. When we were filming in Burnham Beeches I would hear Concord go over and I would look up and say, "Bye-bye Kev, see you on Monday." He always went back home because, as he explained to me on our daily natters, he was trying to get the final touches to his latest film, Dances with Wolves, done. Then came the weekend that he was not going home. He had brought his film back with him and had hired the Cannon Theatre for a private showing of Dances with Wolves for the cast and crew the following Sunday. I got my friend Chris to come up and look after the animals for me and Dal and myself were off to London without a clue where we were going, but we found it. We sat in the top gallery with everyone else, which included lots of famous people who happened to be in London that weekend. Kevin came and stood before us explaining that this was his baby. It had taken him two years to make and he hoped we would enjoy it. He told us that it would be the first time that he had seen it as it had not been released yet. He then came and sat next to Dal and gave me a reassuring pat on the hand. Such a lovely man. The film was fantastic and I was able to appreciate it so much more because I knew such a lot of the inside story of the making of it. Kevin had told me he did all his own stunts and he is a wonderful horse rider. His only one regret was, after spending hours with Two Socks, it was not his hand that Two Socks eventually took the meat from.

After the film, we all left for the Groucho

Club for cocktails and canapés. The streets were lined with photographers waiting to catch the stars. They took one look at me and Dal and decided we were not stars and gave us a miss. We followed Morgan Freeman and his wife because we didn't have a clue where to go. When it was time to leave I went and found Kevin to say thank you and had a lovely kiss on the cheek, a big beaming smile and a, "See you in the morning, Pam." Oh what a lucky, happy bunny I was.

We had a bit of an issue when it came time to leave as we had no idea where we had left the Land Rover. We did eventually find it but then we had to work out how to get out of London. We seemed to be going around in circles but we managed it in the end. Dal and Chris went home and I went to sleep in the luton of my lorry, very happy indeed.

Life back on the farm in January was always very challenging. Everything seemed to take much longer and the bedding down was endless, but the thing that I was really happy about, and had missed greatly, was my log fire and armchair at the end of the day. I used to sit there with my favourite tipple and think how lucky I had been, telling myself that every dog has its day and I had certainly had mine. I was back home with all my wonderful memories and thinking nothing like that would ever happen to me again, and all because my beautiful Dexters had horns.

Kevin Costner with Eileen and me

28. HERE WE GO AGAIN

Winter rolled on to Spring and the start of the showing season and I received a phone call from the same production team that had done Prince of Thieves. I was asked if I still had Fred and Gertie, which I did. They also asked if I had a load of cattle with horns, which I did, and so they asked me if I would like to join them once again on a new production. I was delighted to and this time I asked what film it was and who would be in it. It was called First Knight and would star Sean Connery and Richard Gere.

The first day of filming came around. I had about twelve of my friends and family as extras. This was so they could control the cattle. We were at that location for about four days so we all camped around the set and had a fabulous time. My wranglers, as they were known to the crew, had never done anything like it before and it was just like one big party.

My wranglers on First Knight

I arrived on set two days early to let the cattle get used to their new surroundings. They had built a rustic corral in the middle of the village with no water troughs and no running water so endless buckets of water had to be carried. There were lots of things going on around the set so never a dull moment. I watched men practising their swords skills only to find out later that I had been watching

Richard Gere all afternoon and I didn't have a clue. Well, I didn't know what he looked like, did I?!

The scenes we were involved in were the biggest and most important scenes of the whole film. We were in a purpose built village in the middle of the woods at Ivanhoe.

When all the scenes had been shot and 'in the can' the final scene would be done. This was the big one. The entire village was to be burnt down by marauders. It was hard work as the marauders kept charging the village and scattering the cattle and goats everywhere as none of the animals were ever tied up. They did scene after scene until the director got what he wanted. Getting all the cattle, goats, sheep and chickens back into their positions was not an easy task. The goats were the hardest but we soon learned to leave a length of rope on them. By the end of the shoot we had lost a goat and could not find her anywhere. The forest rangers said they would look out for her and ring me when she was found. I had a phone call two weeks later and went to collect her. Her days of freedom were over!

Eventually they had all the shots they needed and the time came to burn the village down. Cameras were positioned everywhere, some even high on cranes. Fire engines surrounded the village (out of shot) and people and animals fled everywhere. Stunt guys ran around on fire and everyone had dirty faces. The extras all got extra pay that day. It was called 'dirt money'. Now the village was gone and we just hoped the director was happy with what he got.

Filming days and locations were a lot more low key and the majority of the filming was done on purpose built sets at Pinewood Studios. Finally, after four to five months it was completed. I didn't go to the wrap party this time either as I considered that I had already missed the best one and so I gave it a miss.

Four to five months later, the invitation to a cast and crew showing turned up. There were only two tickets so I decided to take my daughter, Lyn, who had helped out on major shoots and kept everything in order at home. We travelled up to London on the Sunday of the screening, meeting at the theatre with old friends from the filming days. We filled the theatre, the organ stopped playing and disappeared down into the stage and the film began. There were no titles, just an aerial shot of the village in the woodland, then the shot panned in on Richard Gere sword fighting, with the villagers looking on.

Richard knocked the other man's sword out of his hand and the camera closed in on Richard. He was smiling almost full screen and there, next to him, were my daughter and I, cheering and smiling.

Well, I couldn't believe it. I had done hours and hours in costume on Prince of

Thieves and never saw myself on screen once, only my hand. I knew it was my hand because it was holding onto two goats and I know I would have given my handlers one goat to hold but not two, so it had to be my hand.

29. DAL'S SLIPOVERS OF MANY COLOURS

Filming my first major film (Prince of Thieves) was a mind boggling experience for me and it took me quite a while to adjust to the filming way of life. I soon learned that there was an awful lot of hanging around and, me being the busy person I had always been, I found myself quite bored (in a funny sort of way!) and I decided I needed some knitting to do.

I had always been a keen knitter, but here I was stuck in the middle of Burnham Beeches with only a lorry for transport and dozens of animals. I managed to get hold of my daughter and told her my sad story about being bored and what I needed her to do.

I told her that in the old oak chest in the sitting room she would find some odd balls of wool that had been left over from garments I had knitted in the years gone by and also a buddle of knitting needles. I said for her to bung it all in a bag and I will sort it out. Dal was making his usual trip to me at the weekend and he arrived with a big dust bin bag full of knitting wool, all colours of the rainbow. Now I had to decide what I was going to knit. I had no pattern so it would have to be simple and I just loved doing fair isle. The next task was to sort out some sort of colour scheme and of course the same thickness of wool was needed. It was going to be hard going to get started and I was prepared that I wouldn't get it right first time but eventually it was all looking good and I was away.

During the day I was always dressed up has a woodland peasant and part of my costume was a big old shawl. I would sit on a log knitting away and keeping an eye on the animals and geese and when they were finally ready to shoot a scene and shout 'cameras rolling' I would drop my Tesco's carrier bag (containing my knitting) on the floor and put my old shawl over the top to hide the offending white bag and be ready by the time they said 'action'.

The first slipover I knitted was really

smart and you would never have thought it was made out of left over balls of wool. The photo I have included is my second attempt and Dal my lovely model husband. When it came to slipovers three and four, they were all the colours of the rainbow but Dal love them and wore them all the time during the winter under his overalls. I still have one in the draw and an old friend, Prudence, asked if she could have one which she wears (actually the one in the photo). Oh, these wonderful memories, no one can take them away ! ! !

30. PIGS THAT NEED TO BE DOGS

In the early stages of one production I was asked if I could train some pigs to walk on leashes or harnesses so, five months before filming was due to start, I bought four Berkshire pigs. Berkshires are black with white points (legs, face and tail). I bought them quite young, at about six weeks old, to try and get them humanised. I also decided to keep them in pairs rather than four in one pack. This was to get them more used to people and so they would be more like dogs. Each one was put on a harness from the very beginning and led around like dogs. The film was The Fifth Element starring Bruce Willis.

It was a futuristic film and, where I usually worked in the past, this was set in the future. I was also asked for two male handlers who would be part of the cast. They had to be tall and have a certain jawline. I sent photos in, which had to be taken from two angles, front and sideways, of their heads. They chose Martin, my son, and Kevin, my son-in-law. They were both over six feet tall and must have had the correct looking jawlines. They had to go for costume fittings where we found out they were going to be policemen with pigs. They had to have helmets specially made to fit and the only bit of their faces showing were their jawlines.

Martin and Kevin with their pigs on Fifth Element

Fitting sessions went on over the next few weeks and they looked a bit like Michelin men. The pig training went on and we definitely had two pigs better than the others. Chain harnesses were made for them and everything was ready. The film was all being made on purpose built sets in Pinewood Studios so I just knew I was going to have a poo and pee problem. It was going to be a nightmare. It would be on painted concrete floors which meant splashing, and the smell would get to everyone and when it was cleaned up thoroughly, the floor would be wet and people might slip. Oh, I wasn't looking forward to it at all. Anyway, we filmed all day with me as chief cleaner-up. Everything seemed to be going fine and everyone was happy. Next morning the buyer came to see me saying they had run through yesterday's filming with the director Luc Besson, who had been working on another set all that precious day, and he said he wanted bigger pigs. I said that's as big as they are and I would not be able to get bigger ones that would walk on harnesses this late in the day. He went back to the powers-that-be and it was decided that the pigs would be dropped and the boys would be given guns instead. My poo nightmare was over and the boys were more than happy with their guns and, as an extra bonus, every time they fired the guns they got extra payment at the end of the day. The pigs went home and I was given a part to play, so everyone was happy.

31. THE SHOW MUST GO ON

I was down in Cornwall filming with a French film crew, doing a Treasure Island production. One evening, after being on set all day, I arrived at the farm of a friend to put all the animals to bed. It had rained all day and was still pouring. Rushing to get it all done and get into the warmth and out of my wet clothes, I was crossing some rough ground with half a sack of pig nuts and a bucket of water when I caught my foot on a green plastic wire hidden in the grass and I went sprawling downhill and landed really heavily on the stone track. I had broken my shoulder. They strapped me up at hospital and I was again on set the next morning. Luckily I had four helpers with me so they were able to drive and do the heavy work. I endured a week of pain then I went home and went to my hospital as instructed by Truro Hospital. They kept me in and said they would operate and put a plate in my shoulder. Well, they were unable to plate it as it was so badly smashed. They just took some floating bone away. The pain after the operation was just awful and we were just about to move out of our beloved farm house to have a barn conversion done on what was now our new main farm. The plan was to live in a wooden shed while the barn was being converted. All the packing-up had to be done and with only one arm I was not a lot of use, so I had to rely on my daughters to do most of the work.

It was April and we had finally moved out of the farmhouse on the opposite side of the road and into our wooden shed. We had electricity but no running water. Adjacent to the shed was one of my caravans I used on film sets. We would sleep in that. We still had our old sign from our first original home, DALAPAM, so we nailed that above our entrance (forty years later). Life was still moving on. The plan was that the barn conversion would be finished by Christmas. I was still filming but couldn't drive as it was my left shoulder that was strapped to my body so I couldn't change gear. We got by and it wouldn't be for long, so I thought!

Then it happened. I had a day or two off from the set. I was working on Atonement with Keira Knightley and there were lots of days when I was not needed which was suiting me fine at that moment because the pain in my shoulder was still awful and some nights I hardly slept.

It was early September and Dal and I decided to go and pick some apples in the field at the back of the church. I walked down the lane and Dal came with the little old tractor and link box and plastic bags to fill with apples. We had a lovely afternoon and Dal remarked that, at last, I was getting better. All those pain killers were not good. He drove out of the little orchard, into the big one where the cattle were grazing. He suggested that I stand in the link box with the bags of apples so I climbed on board and held on with my right hand. Dal shouted over his shoulder, "We will go and see how the walnut tree is doing." I thought I would rather go and have a cup of tea. When we got to the tree he slowed down and I let go so I could step out backwards. At that moment Dal took his foot off the clutch. The tractor was still in gear and shot forwards, flinging me out the back of the link box which was still off the ground. There I was, on my back, on the floor. The pain was unbearable and I was making lots of noise to try and relieve it. My mobile phone was in the pocket of my shorts so Dal took it and rang 999. I was trying to tell him he had to unlock the phone but he had gotten through on the emergency number. He was explaining what had happened and the woman on the line was asking for our location. He was explaining, "You come down Church Lane to Moreton Valence church, through the church yard, through the kissing gate, round the moat and over the style," and within minutes a paramedic arrived and was giving me gas and air but it wasn't easing the pain.

A helicopter was flying overhead but it went away because there was nowhere for it to land. The ambulance arrived and the driver was shown by Dal how to get in through the tractor entrance. I had been given the maximum amount of morphine and still the pain was unbearable. They needed to get me on a spinal board but every slightest movement was agony. Off I went to hospital yet again. The verdict was a broken right wrist, a badly shattered shoulder and cracked sternum. When I finally came home from hospital the builders greeted me and said there had been a special delivery for me and they had put it in what we were calling the "love shack." I thought, "That's nice. Who would have sent me flowers?" Having real difficulty in walking, with no arms for balance wasn't easy but I made my way to my little dwelling place only to find that the delivery was a commode, a long handled hairbrush and extensions to go on knives and forks and no flowers! What a predicament to get myself into. My right arm was plastered to within one inch of the end of my fingers and in a sling, my left arm was completely strapped to my body, and I couldn't do anything for myself.

The next morning I was due at the hospital again and Dal was trying to get me washed and dressed. I was stood, leaning my back against a chest of drawers for balance. It was time to change my knickers, dirty ones off and clean ones on. Dal was pulling them up and I was telling him they didn't feel right. He realised that one of my legs was going through the waist of the knickers and the leg opening was around my waist. We were both laughing our heads off. Dal was on his knees with my knickers half on and half off when the door to our shed opened and our daughter-in-law appeared, wondering if we needed any help. We all eventually stopped laughing and got on with the job in hand. Oh, we did have our moments but we can honestly say we never once fell out. It was ten months before I was able to drive. We should have bought an automatic vehicle but I just kept thinking I would soon be better and, to be honest, it was nice being driven around.

32. HONEY BEES AND FROGS

During the filming of Atonement I was asked for some honey bees. I enquired what the scene was and was told it was just really to establish that it was a hot sunny day in summer and that the bees were needed on some flowers and maybe one in the window where they were filming from, out towards the garden. So, I had to get my thinking cap on again, because I couldn't really think of a way of doing it. I went along to a honey extracting plant not too far from me, to pick their brains and, believe it or not, it all became rather simple. Apparently, the frames full of honey get collected from the hives out in the orchards. They always have a number of bees still in them and when they are unloaded and put in stacks inside the processing building they eventually make their way out of the frame and fly towards the light which shines through the many windows. They are known as lost bees and are doomed to die, as even if they were let out, they would never find their way back to the hive. I was told I could collect as many as I wanted from the windows but they would only live for about six to eight hours, so on the given day I arranged to pick some up at 6:00am and travel to the film set. I stored them in a maggot box with ventilation holes with a bit of honey in one corner and a drop of water and put them in a cool, shady spot. Just before they were needed I transferred about four of them into a small water bottle, that I had swilled out with water with the idea that they would fly around the bottle and get their wings damp so when I placed them on the flowers they would not be able to fly away until their wings were dry enough. The same practise was put in place for the window scene. They just crawled around the window pane. It worked really well and the remainder of the bees at the end of the day were given their freedom.

I then got a call from my buyer on

Atonement asking if I could sort them some frogs for the following week. I asked how many and they said that they only wanted one, not a big one (quite small really). By that time I knew how directors could be and I imagined being told they wanted a bigger frog or a smaller frog than the frog I picked. You never can really read their minds and you can't simply change the size of the frog so I decided to find a number of frogs of varying sizes to be on the safe side.

It was summer time and we were having a dry spell and frogs don't come out when it's dry. I have a friend who I rely on for my frogs so I rang her that night and asked Di what the chances were of getting some frogs. She hadn't seen any for ages so we decided to see if we could trick some frogs into coming out by making them think it was raining. We would do this using a hosepipe and sprinkler over Di's pond. After three nights we had six frogs. This was when I was only half in action because of my arm injuries. The shot was in Norfolk, three hours away, and it was an afternoon shoot so I was asked to go for lunch time and was told it shouldn't take long. So, Martin and I arrived with the frogs safe

and sound in a make-do aquarium. Joe
Wright, the director, grabbed us as they were
about to break for lunch and said he'd take
me and show me the shot he wanted before
lunch, so off we went across some fields and
came to a rheam (a still water gulley) with a
make shift raft on the water and small wild lily
pads around it. Joe pointed to a lily pad and
said that he wanted a frog on that lily pad,
which was about ten foot away from the bank.
I asked if we could work from the raft but
that was for the camera man who must keep
very still because they didn't want any ripples
on the water. We had to do it all from the
side. He then went for lunch and Martin and I
talked about how we were going to do it. We
had a landing net that we could tie a plastic
water bottle to. The water bottle would have
its bottom cut out and the frog placed inside.
Martin would have a rope around his waist
and the prop boys would hold him so he
could lean out over the water and carefully
drop the frog down on the pad. I told him to
go and get his lunch and I went to the back of
the catering van and asked one of the boys if
they had some ice cubes that I could have. My
luck was in and off I went to our truck armed
with a bag of ice cubes. I dropped them in the

water, one by one, with the frogs perched on the rocks and weeds looking at me. I then covered the whole aquarium trying to get the temperature inside down. I then went and joined Martin for lunch and told him what his clever mum had done, to which I received one of his nice smiles. When lunch was over we all made our way back to the set. Everything was ready, the camera was rolling and everyone was looking. The frog was in the bottle and Martin had it suspended over the water. The frog was encouraged to leave the bottle and with success he landed on the pad but the wrong way round with his back to the camera. That was no good so we reloaded the bottle with Martin asking if we could put him in the way we wanted him to come out but that would never work because the bottle had to be held up in the air until we were ready to lower it again and the frog could simply move while up there. On the second go, with the camera rolling, we held our breaths and the frog came out the right way round. Joe smiled but then he asked me if I could poke the frog as he didn't look real. He wasn't moving. I told Joe if he waited a moment the frog would warm up. Everyone was laughing and at that second the frogs eyelids moved, his throat bobbed and he leapt off the lily pad. Cheers went up and our mission was accomplished. We went home very happy with a job well done.

When the film came out we found that that scene had been scrapped. The editor must have decided it was not needed.

When a film is made, it usually takes five months of filming and the editor is given about one hundred hours of film which then has to be cut down to about a two hour film, so a lot of our work never gets shown.

Where, on the other hand, if it's TV work, all of our bloopers get shown on It'll Be

Alright on the Night and I have had quite a few of those, but then that is what makes my job so enjoyable.

33. DOWN TO EARTH

We had quite of a lot of those bloopers on Down to Earth. The lovely Pauline Quirke was a joy to work with. I was so lucky to have someone with such a good sense of humour and you definitely needed that when working with animals and poor Pauline had her fill of them over the years.

To start with, there were the family's two dogs, Parsley and Honey. Parsley, the male dog, loved Pauline from day one, which was fine because on set they were so natural together. He was always so pleased to see her, would always greet her as she arrived in a car and he was really eager to follow her anywhere, which made my job easy. The two of them were inseparable which meant I could concentrate on other things.

One day, we had a bedroom scene. Pauline was in bed and Parsley's role was to knock the bedroom door open, run in and jump on the bed and greet Pauline. Well, as per usual, one take wasn't enough. I think we were on the third one, Parsley was getting hot and excited and came bouncing in, up on the bed and sprawled over Pauline and started doing what no decent male would do in public. Well, that was another one for It'll Be Alright on the Night. Then there was the time when it was decided the family needed a cow and Pauline went to market to buy one. She arrived back home, cow in trailer. The tailboard came down, Pauline walked up into the trailer, untied the cow to walk out with her but the cow decided she wanted to come out first with Pauline tagging on. Not quite what the director wanted so we ended up doing that scene quite a few times, changing the angle of the camera so I was in the trailer talking sweet nothings in the cows ear and Pauline was able to bring out her latest purchase with pride and show her bemused family but who was going to milk it?!

Then there were the pigs. Another addition to the farm and more problems to be solved. The storyline was that Pauline, for one reason or another, had gotten locked out of the house one night and the only place for her to sleep was with the pigs. How to get the scene? After quite a bit of thought it was decided there'd be a nice clean pig-sty with lots of straw and some heat lights over where they wanted to shoot. The pigs would go for a nice walk, get a nice feed and water and then be encouraged to lie down in the right positions and go to sleep, which you can do by tickling and rubbing their bellies. There was Marion, my helper, on one side concentrating on one pig and me on the other. The crew was deadly silent and Pauline came in while the pigs were asleep, hoping there was enough room for her between them. The whole thing went absolutely perfectly.

When I was first given the contract for Down to Earth all of the filming was around London. What a rude awaking that was for me. I had never driven in London. Every day was a different location and in those days there was no satnav so I only had an A to Z. I managed it though and felt quite proud of myself. If anyone had told me I would be driving around London at fifty-five years old I would have said, "No way!"

The next big task was to find a Jersey cow that all the family could milk and Rosemary, the producer, said that she must be very quiet, so, after lots of searching, I found the perfect cow, Maisey.

Me, Maisey and Flickling

Rosemary came to inspect her. "Pam," she said, "she is lovely but her eyes are not dark enough." You could have knocked me down with a feather. After gathering myself together I told Rosemary that Maisey would do everything that she wanted; stand like a rock, let two people milk her at the same time and let you pump her tail for milk and, "Anyway," I said, "I think she's got lovely eyes!" Rosemary agreed but still said that they weren't black enough around the eyes so it was then decided that we would make her eyes up much darker before Maisey went in front of the camera. Daphne the make-up girl was summoned, make-up was applied to Maisey's eyes and Rosemary was happy. Maisey had her own make-up bag and her own personal make-up girl called Daphne.

The next task, later on in filming, Maisey had to have a calf but she wasn't even in calf in real life, so four in-calf cows were brought to the film set, all of them due to calf within a ten day period, so one was due to produce to suit a slot in the filming programme. Every time a cow was about to give birth I would inform production and say, "About two hours and we will have a calf." "Oh, sorry Pam, it won't be today, we are too busy." Came the response and so it went on until after the third calf was born. I was now jumping up and down saying that they would only have one more chance at this scene. We were down to our last cow and I couldn't just go and buy any more off the shelf at Marks & Spencer's. So, all the stops were pulled out and they got what they wanted. It was late on the Saturday evening when the calf was finally born and everyone found it very emotional with tears all around, even from some of the men. When the cameras stopped rolling a quick inspection confirmed it was a male calf. "Oh dear," I said, "it's a boy." Everyone went home very late that night and not due in until Monday morning. The next morning I rang the farmer who owned the cow and he came and collected her and her new born from the set. Monday morning, the crew were asking me why I had said, "oh dear," when I had found out that the calf was a boy, to which I answered quite honestly, "boys are of no use and are slaughtered." The crew were horrified. Next thing I knew I was confronted by Rosemary asking if what I had said was true. I simply nodded to which she responded by saying that I must go and buy it as everyone was up in arms about it. I said it was probably too late, that the knackerman might have already collected it but I rang the farmer anyway and asked him if he still had the calf. He did, but the knackerman was due any minute so I asked him not to let it go and I bought it from him and I became the keeper of quite a useless animal. Useless but very cute, called Choccy by the crew.

The following year Choccy was written into the script only to be killed off by anthrax when it was discovered on the farm and that was the end of Choccy's filming career but Maisey was used quite a bit on other jobs.

While on Down to Earth I was asked to make it look as though Parsley had eaten a mobile phone so, after some thought, we came up with a plan using toffees and liquorice laces. They wanted Parsley to be chewing like mad and swallowing, with the wire from the phone charger hanging from his mouth. So, on cue, Marion would chew a toffee, get it all nice and gooey, attach a length of liquorice to it and ram it between Parsley's back teeth, not allowing him to chew until action was called. It worked a treat and after about three takes we had the shot. We also had dribble everywhere. Another satisfying day.

In one series of Down to Earth I was asked for a pony that Molly, the family's young daughter, could ride. This was fine and there was no problem finding a nice quiet pony for her and, at my suggestion, we were to have a companion for Molly's pony. I had just the perfect one at home on the farm. My granddaughter, Lily, who was 3 years old at the time had a lovely little black and white Shetland pony called Poppet and she was adorable. Everything with the two ponies was a huge success but as the weeks went by I was getting a little bit concerned because Poppet was getting very overweight and I didn't want her to get laminitis which ponies get when they are getting too much grass. At night time, after filming, I would pen her on a small strip of ground with almost no grass on it with just a bucket of water, telling her it was for her own good as she would not like to get laminitis. We had a two week break from filming due so all the animals were loaded up and we made the trip home. While at home Poppet was still on her diet. It was easier at home as she was kept in the yard with limited hay which was better than summer flush of grass. Well, talk about getting it wrong. I most certainly had gotten it completely wrong. I got up bright and early one morning, going from one job to another and finally got to the stable yard where I could not believe my eyes as, there in the yard, was the cutest tiny black and white baby foal standing next to its mother. From that moment onwards Poppet was given the very best of food with me telling her I was so sorry I got it wrong. We had only owned Poppet for about six months and was not told that she might be pregnant. In actual fact she was five months in foal when she came to us. He was quickly given the name Zeebee because Lily had a plastic pony on wheels with a black and white rug on and he was known as Zeebee and she thought the world of him and so now Lily had a real Zeebee. I now had a dilemma because continuity is everything in filming and we still had lots of filming to do. I rang production and told them the story of little Zeebee and he was written into the script. Everyone loved him, he was completely spoilt and got away with blue murder.

He roamed freely on the set if we were filming with his mum and would keep running back to her and then off to find more mischief.

Zeebee

If he wandered too far away the lads would pick him up and return him to his mum. It wasn't long until he started nibbling and that was bad news for the boys because all the male film crew wore shorts and that naughty little boy first started tugging at their shorts and nibbling their boot laces and then he found the bare flesh at the back of their legs and when they weren't looking and everything was quiet you would suddenly hear, "Ouch!!"

And then we come right back to talking

about poo. We have definitely had our moments as the one thing that animals do quite often is poo. On Down to Earth they suddenly announced they would like a goat in a bedroom scene. It was the end of the day and not scheduled as far as I was concerned but I fetched a goat and went up the stairs as requested. The poor goat got confused as she had never been up the stairs before. They were winding and the steps very narrow at one end and so she started pooing and you all surely know that goats poo is like little currants that go everywhere. They ended up bouncing from one step to another, all the way down the stairs and everybody trod on them. The scene was meant to be Pauline in bed, asleep, with the goat nibbling her nose to wake her. Well, the goat didn't get it quite right and we were running out of time, so we would call it a wrap and planned to redo that scene first thing in the morning.

Me and some of the goats from First Knight

That evening we played games with the goat, going up and down the stairs until she thought it was great fun and we were able to call it a day. We had to see to all the other animals and to ourselves and hopefully play a game or two of Rummicup before bed. Marion and I lived in a caravan on set and always liked to end our day with a couple of games. Next morning we were ready and waiting with the goat. "Okay, goat please Pam, and no poo this morning," they said. I replied, "Sorted" and someone asked what I meant by that. I looked at Marion and said for her to show them. Marion took two corks out of her pocket. They looked shocked and passed on the information from one to another until the whole crew were convinced we had done the necessary deed. The scene went without a hitch, with no poo and a big cheer went up. We then had to try and explain that we hadn't done what they all thought we had done. Trying to convince them that it would never work was a really hard job as they preferred to think it was the corks that had intervened.

When we did the first series of Down to Earth we never knew for sure if there would be a second series the following year. We had to wait until it viewed on television to see what the ratings were like. Well, the audience loved it and we were granted another series. Everything was in the planning stages when foot and mouth broke out. There was no way we could go to the farm in Devon so it was then planned to build all the inside sets at Twickenham Studios. Being as I lived on our farm, I had to leave with the dogs in case our farm got closed down. So, me and Parsley and Honey went to live with Marion in Dorridge until they started filming in Twickenham. We spent about two months in the studios. We were coming to the end of all the inside scenes and there was no sign of foot and mouth ending. In the end we were granted permission to go to Devon but we had to set up a large disinfection plant in and out of the film set. That way we were able to get on with the job in hand and, one way or another, the series got finished.

The following year the storyline had changed somewhat, and a purpose built set was established at Henley-on-Thames, miles from the busy road and on the edge of a wood. It was like paradise and everyone that visited the set wanted to live there. We set up home there for the five months of filming and I was set with yet again many more challenges but all very enjoyable. We had Red Kites circling about us. The estate was also used to rear pheasants and some of the woods were fenced off for this purpose. The gamekeeper was always doing his rounds. In the beginning of the pheasant rearing they have quite a few die and they are flung over the fence for the Red Kites. Red Kites only take dead stock so this is what attracted them to this spot. They are a lovely sight gliding gracefully, circling with their beautiful wing span and 'V' shaped tails.

I was also introduced to the Henley Regatta and at weekends there were concerts in the park with wonderful firework displays. Life was very good indeed. We were just like one big happy family that met up ever spring to do another series. Of course, they all went home at weekends but for me it was better for the animals that we stayed in situ. Everyone would tell me what they got up to at weekends at home with their families and I would have my family coming to visit me and bring me clean clothes, post and anything I needed and maybe extra animals or changing some over and it all worked out lovely.

It was a five year contract that I had for Down to Earth which came on the TV screens each autumn, each being twelve or so episodes in length.

Me & Cast and crew from Down to Earth

34. PERIOD DRAMAS

While all of the film work and TV dramas were happening I had the TV people telephoning me as they were looking for animals for their period dramas. It was a time when television period dramas were popular.

One of the most stressful of these productions I did was Far From the Maddening Crowd. It was summer time and they wanted lots of sheep, all in their full fleeces, not trimmed. It was a hot summer and not ideal for moving sheep around, especially ones that had not been shorn. It was mainly shot in the lovely up hill and down dale countryside of Derbyshire. One evening, after a long day of filming, I collected my call sheet for the next day to check on what animals they required, hoping that I had all that was needed. I loaded up the lorry and made for the next location.

A nearby farm had agreed to take the sheep overnight. I was on my own, trying to read the map and drive. As I was approaching a railway bridge, I saw that I needed to turn right just after the bridge so I swung a little to the left to get my lock on to turn right and "crunch" I hit the top of the bridge on the passenger side. The engine stalled so I started it up again and tried to reverse out from under the bridge but I was completely wedged in. The engine stalled again. A man came to my rescue and tried standing on the passenger step to weight the cab down but that failed so there was only one alternative - to let the passenger tyre down until we could release the cab. It was successful and I was again on my way, only this time with a flat tyre and no power steering. The road was narrow, very bendy and steep but eventually I got to my overnight stay. The farmyard was full of rubbish and broken down machinery. There was nowhere really to turn. The farmer came to show me where to put the sheep. The plan was to turn the lorry around, reverse to the shed and then it would be safe to unload and reload in the morning. So I started to turn around but it was easier said than done. Backwards then forwards, brake on and off all of the time because we were on a hill. Backwards and forwards it went on, me being directed by the farmer. The cab started filling up with smoke fumes. We had to get this lorry turned and the farmer was saying that we were nearly there. Thank God, please God I kept saying. I was at the end of my tether. My lorry had a flat tyre. I had now burnt the clutch out and I was miles from anywhere. I unloaded the sheep and fed and watered them and I then tried to ring Dal but he didn't (or wouldn't) carry a mobile phone so I had to catch him when he came into the house. I knew he was haymaking so I just rang every twenty minutes or so. He finally answered the phone and I could pour my heart out to him, but he stopped me before I had a chance to say anything. He had just fetched himself fish and chips and wanted to eat them before they got cold. "Ring back in ten minutes," he'd said. That was the last straw and I burst into tears.

My son Martin travelled up to the film set very early the next morning. He brought me a

new load of sheep in the Land Rover and
trailer and I continued with the day's filming
as he went to sort out my lorry. Later that day
it was back in action. I hadn't burnt the
clutch. It had just gotten a bit warm, then so
did I!

Me and Gizmo on Vanity Fair

I was lucky to get landed with the
production of Pride & Prejudice, starring
Keira Knightley, Donald Sutherland and Judi

Dench. There were lots of animals needed, a special dog called Buzz, a herd of Longhorn cattle and loads of ducks that had to be on the moat around the family house.

Buzz was the most wonderful dog working for me. He was a deerhound and a real gentleman with so much dignity. I was always losing him and he could always be found in a comfy chair or asleep next to someone who was having a break. Buzz earned quite a bit of money for his owner and she announced that she was buying him Premium Bonds with it and when he won, he could buy a lovely house and she would go to live with him. I wonder if his numbers ever came up!

The set for Pride & Prejudice was at Groombridge. Groombridge Place was an old large 17th Century manor house. It had a large moat going around it. It was suggested that I moved in about seven days before filming to get the animals settled before all of the hustle and bustle started. One of the big features was going to be the ducks on the moat. I thought it strange that there seemed to be no life at all on the moat, not even fish. I released the

ducks thinking they would be really happy
there and went about my other jobs. I was set
up with two caravans away from the actual
house so I was out of shot. Quite late that
evening I went to check the ducks and have a
head count and to my horror I had three dead
ducks with their heads eaten off. They were
up on large planks of wood that were put
across the moat to walk on. I had the
telephone number of the caretaker if I needed
anything so I rang him to say what had
happened. "That will be the mink," he said.
No-one had told me there was mink in the
water. He said they'd always had trouble with
them. They'd had the mink catchers out but
they couldn't catch them. I had found a
battered cage in a shed that I had cleaned out
for the chickens, so I thought if I could mend
the cage I might be able to catch one. I got
the cage and fixed it and put a duck carcass in
it and placed it on the plank where the blood
still was. I had also tied a rope onto the cage
because I knew if I was lucky enough to catch
one there was no way I could pick the cage up
without losing a couple of fingers. I went back
to the caravan, taking the two other carcasses
with me. An hour later, I went back down
with a torch to check my trap and I had a

 mink in it. I rang the caretaker and between us we disposed of it. I went on catching them until they were all gone and I was able to release the ducks again.

We were set up at Groombridge for quite a while as a lot of the story was set around the family's house and property. One scene was set in the wonderful large kitchen and they had scripted a very large pig, a Gloucester Old Spot, to walk through the kitchen. Well, the largest friendly pig I could find was signed up for the job. The day was set for the shoot. It was summer time and very hot for transporting a large pig in an aluminum trailer, so it was planned that Dal and Tom would leave our farm at 2:30am and travel the four hours to Groombridge in the coolness of the early morning and get there in time for 7:00am breakfast and sunrise. At 11:00pm that night, I had a phone call from the 2nd assistant to the director asking if I had heard what happened to Judi Dench that day. I hadn't. I was told that she was stung by a wasp quite badly on the face and her scenes had been dropped for tomorrow and therefore we wouldn't need the pig. I tried ringing Dal but he had gone to bed and I I've said before, he would not carry a mobile phone so I wondered how I was going to stop him. I tried ringing Tom. There was no answer on the house phone so then I rang his mobile and, after what seemed like forever, he answered. It was decided that Tom would go to the farm as planned at 2:00am and tell my husband that it was all off for the day. I knew Dal would not be amused and I was very pleased that dear Tom would tell him and not me. Good old Tom. Anyway, we did the pig scene a few days later and everyone was happy once more.

Groombridge was a lovely time for me. It was a wonderful setting with lots to see and do on days off. In the evening we would take the dogs for lovely walks into the woods and for the first time since I was a small child I found glowworms. I remember as a child, Dad would carry me on his shoulders, coming home from friends that we used to visit on Notwood Hill. We took a short cut over Huntley Hill and Dad would pick the glowworms up and give them to me to carry home. When we arrived home I would put the glowworms on the lawn beneath my bedroom window and before I got into bed I would look at them from the window and then all those years later I found glowworms at Groombridge. That was about twelve or thirteen years ago and I have never seen one since. I would love to think I may again see them somewhere.

We had some fun with geese while filming Wives & Daughters. We had to take ten geese to Bath where they were needed for a scene that was to be shot on a road next to the thermal spa. For those of you who don't know Bath, it's in the centre of the city and the scene was to be filmed on a Saturday afternoon.

Hanging around in the streets of Bristol

"Hey, We're Here!"

The geese were loaded into the trailer at the farm and off we went. My wrist was still not fully healed after my accident on the tractor so Eileen came along to help. Knowing that we wouldn't be able to park close to the location Eileen asked how we were going to get the geese, which were loose in the trailer, from the trailer to the location. "We'll just walk them there," I said. When

Eileen reminded me that the city centre would be bustling with shoppers on a Saturday afternoon I simply replied, "Well, they'll just have to get out of the way then."

We parked as close as we could to where they were filming but it was still quite a long way away. Anyway, right there in the middle of a busy shopping area, with masses of people milling about, we lowered the trailer tailboard and out waddled the geese, as good as gold. I walked in front and they followed me with Eileen keeping them moving from behind and they went exactly where we needed them to go.

The bemused shoppers parted like the Red Sea to let them through. Some were clearly scared of them, other just curious. The geese, well, they were completely unfazed and went on to play their part in the filming like true professionals, getting a rousing round of applause from the cast and crew as they were rounded up to go home.

I have done two Tess of the d'Urbervilles over the years, both very challenging, as we had to have lots of cows, all quiet enough for the artists to hand-milk, although a lot of the time we could fake it.

One shot was in the milking shed with about ten cows tied up in the milking bays with ten milkmaids sat on stools, milking. A running track ran the whole length of the set behind the cows and milkmaids. The director started stating what he wanted. "Pam, first cow two inches forward. Pam, second cow two inches back, third cow okay" and so it went on, then, "Reposition the milkmaids." He was aiming to see all the milkmaids milking as the camera came along the track, then the camera was to fix on Tess milking but the cow kept swishing her tail so, with me on my knees, just out of camera frame, I held onto part of her tail. Oh, my poor knees, no wonder I've had to have a new one.

Milk maids on Tess of the d'Urbervilles

In another scene the director wanted Gabriel milking a cow and lose his concentration on the milking when looking at

Tess. He wanted the cow to knock the bucket of milk over. I told him that we train our cows not to kick and he said that was the scene so we had to do it somehow. He also said that he wanted a trial run before lunch so he knew where to set the camera up without the milk going over it. We did it in the open yard because it was such a tight close up and the camera man would be lying on his belly. I said that I could probably get her to do it once by poking the back of her heel but doing it twice with exactly the same response couldn't be guaranteed. Anyway, we had a trial run with no camera and it worked perfectly so it was marked where the camera would be set up. I went to lunch convinced that the afternoon would be a disaster. The camera was set up, the cow brought in, Gabriel sat on his stool, the bucket full of milk was brought in and placed under the cow's udder and I was waiting with the offending stick. With the camera rolling and action called I poked her heel and I'm sure I shut my eyes and prayed and when I looked there was milk everywhere and luckily none on the camera. Gabriel was still sitting on his stool, smiles all around and I could breathe again.

Mark, one of the prop guys, trying to come to an understanding with one of the cows on Tess

In the second Tess I was told that it was really important that Gabriel learned to milk, so I suggested that he took milking lessons on a goat because they are much easier as a goat is milked from a milking block and comes up to your level. When he had gotten the knack of milking then he could progress to sitting on a stool next to a cow, doing it all blind by feeling under her for her udder. Cows like you to be close, to put your head into their flank and rub their leg and talk to them. They then feel nice and secure and usually let the milk down quite freely with no fidgeting or kicking. So I arranged for Gabriel, played by Eddie Redmayne, to meet me at a friend's goat farm. We had a lot of fun and he soon got the hang of it. Now we could move on to the cow. He was a natural and had no problems so we were away. I think he was quite proud of himself and so he should be as some people can never get the hang of it.

Gradually, the period dramas were phasing out and because of all the animal licensing and passport control it wasn't that easy to move animals from one location to another. My last big production was Lark Rise to Candleford which ran for four years.

Lark Rise to Candleford was one of the nicest productions I worked on. It was close enough for me to travel home each night and not too many animals to cope with. The biggest stars were the geese. I played the goose lady.

The geese appeared whenever we were filming at Candleford and spent hours standing around the street waiting for their cue for action. They were really the most incredible creatures and would stand around me in a gang and never attempt to wander as long as I was looking at them. If I started staring around or talking they were on the

Me as The Goose Lady

move, like naughty children. They were mostly required to walk down the street and turn to the right with me quite a distance behind them and no one in front. They had to do their own thing. They could have walked straight on or turned left. There was nothing to stop them, but the lovely creatures always turned right and out of shot so I was able to collect them up and go back to number one position for yet another take. Someone once asked me why the geese always turned right. I just looked at them with a very straight face and said, "Because I told them to." We had a good laugh about it when she realised I was joking. My animals did some amazing things for me. I was so lucky. They helped so much to make my job easier than I ever imagined. It was suggested I change my name to Tarzana.

Lark Rise was the poor village. They only had chickens running around and a pig that they were fattening. One day they came to me and asked if it was possible to have a chicken up on one of the roof tops, and would it be able to stay there while the villagers attempted to catch it? I said yes as long as I can be up there with it. That would be fine as I could hide behind the roof on some scaffolding.

On the given day my special chicken was chosen and as a bonus we had a nice day for it. Unbeknown to me a stunt man had been booked for the shoot and came up on the roof with me and the chicken. On 'action' the chicken was placed on the crest of the roof and encouraged to walk along it. She was acting like king of the castle and very much at home. I had nothing to do apart from ask her to move across the roof from one position to another. Everyone thought she was so clever and wanted to stroke her and tell her how good she was. The stunt man had a very easy task that day and we both enjoyed our time in the sun.

Martin on Tom Jones

Me with Eileen and Dal filming Vanity Fair in Chatham Docks

35. A LITTLE TOO MUCH CIDER

We did a live show called Food Fight for television. They asked for two cows that could be hand milked by the contestants. It was in a studio with an audience. There were lots of games all connected with food and the cow milking was going to be the climax of the show. Although it appeared to go on television as a live show it was all pre-recorded and edited, so we knew it was going to be a late one. We were given a dressing room but, having cattle to look after, the dressing room was of no use to us, so we were out the back of the studio with the lorry and cows. There were three of us going to be on set; me, Dal and Jackie. Dal and Jackie leading the Dexter cows and me giving the milking demonstration. We were dressed up as country yokels in breeches and smocks. I was fitted with a microphone as I was doing the talking and I was asked to speak in a broad country accent. I thought, I can't really do that. I speak quite broad anyway and if I tried to make it any worse it would not sound right. We were all acting the fool at being country folks as requested. Jackie produced some cider. No-one knew we were drinking it as it was mixed with Lucozade. The longer the night went on the more we drank so by the time we were called on stage we were the perfect country idiots, with rosy cheeks, big smiles on our faces and certainly a twinkle in my eye. I was required to sit on a stool next to a cow and every time I looked up at the compere I almost fell off the back of it. I had to explain the technique of milking a cow. I started by saying I had a secret ingredient and put my hand down by the side of my stool to feel for it. I couldn't find it. "Someone's pinched it," I said. I looked across to a prop guy and noticed that he had it. He shot it across the floor to me and I actually caught it. The surprised look on my face was a delight as I never catch anything. It was a small pot of

Vaseline for greasing my hands. My little secret. I explained it helps with the action of milking. After rubbing the Vaseline into my hands I demonstrated with my finger and thumb the action require to be able to get the milk out of the teats. The laughing and joking was hilarious but then it was time for the competition. The team with the most milk in the bucket was the winner. It was a huge success and everyone was in a very jolly mood. We were invited to a drinks party but we were more interested in getting home. Travelling home, we were very tired but very pleased with how it had gone. Dal drove and I kept talking to keep him awake. There was no way I was fit to drive although I am sure that cocktail of cider and Lucozade was just what I needed to enhance my performance and my broad, slurry accent. I later received an uncut version of that night's filming with a big thank you. It was hilarious and I couldn't believe it was really me. Oh what happy memories!

Another game show I was asked to do was You Bet. Again the contestants needed to milk a cow. This time the contestants were celebrities who would answer questions and, at the end, the loser would have to do a forfeit. The loser didn't know what the forfeit would be and it was a live show. The loser that night was the lovely Dale Winton. The stage was prepared for the climax of the evening. The plan was for the big doors at the back of the stage to open and a red carpet, which I had requested because I didn't want the cow slipping on the shiny wooden floor, would be rolled out and we would walk in. I had asked if the audience would be quiet and not cheer as we entered. Dal led our lovely little cow in and I walked by her side, carrying a bucket and stool. The audience had no idea what was going to enter but as soon as they saw us they started "oo-ing and aww-ing." The louder the "oos and awws" got I could feel my smile getting wider. At the end of the carpet stood Dale Winton in a frilly apron and a blindfold. The cow stopped and I put the stool down by her. I then took Dale's hand and told him he was going to sit down on a stool. When he was seated with the bucket between his knees, I took his hand and we reached under the cow for her teats. As his hand touched the teats he gave out such a scream. The cow jumped with all four legs off the floor and landed on the polished woodwork, sprawled on her belly with Dal on his knees trying to hold onto her. They collected themselves up and came back on to the carpet. Dale had taken his blindfold off and came to make a fuss of the cow. They were soon friends and he had a go at milking her and everything ended well and, what's more, she didn't do a poo so that was another night when we drove home feeling very very happy with ourselves and proud of our beloved Dexters.

36. CHARLIE THE TURKEY

Another enjoyable production was The Green Green Grass. Again, I could travel home every evening and I was asked for a variety of animals. A firm favourite was Charlie the turkey.

The noise that he made caused quite a stir with the cast and crew. One of the stars recorded his gobbling and used it as his ring tone on his mobile phone. Charlie was a stag bird and used to strut around the film set, in full display, just looking for a potential female. Once they were filming a low-to-the-ground shot and the camera man was on his knees with the camera on a track when the next thing we knew Charlie was on top of the camera man's back and everyone was laughing their heads off. (I think it must have been his aftershave).

I used Charlie in lots of productions and

he became quite famous. He was also used by a company as their Christmas card. This entailed doing a photo shoot in London. The end result was brilliant. He was coming out of an old timber shed wearing glasses, head held high and strutting out full of importance. Good old Charlie!

37. RATS GALORE

One species of animal that I was always asked for was the rat and not your typical pet like rat with the white fur and pink eyes. Oh no, they always wanted the wild looking type.

I soon found a lovely man called David who could provide me with what I was looking for. The rats he had just looked like wild farmyard rats to me but he assured me that he bred them and that they were friendly. Thankfully, he was very professional and I could leave him to get on with his rat scenes with very little help from me.

I first employed David "The Ratman" as I called him on Prince of Thieves. We had rats running everywhere, in the sewers and at the time, I had a young girl, Abbie, working with me. She was fascinated with the rats and was soon helping out. Unfortunately one of the running prisoners in one scene, trod on one of the rats and killed it. Abbie was so upset, she carried this warm, soft, furry body around with her and kept stroking it, willing it to come back to life. Later, when all the filming with the rats had finished and they were being put back in their cages, Abbie took the dead rat out of her pocket and said 'goodbye' to her little friend. She had carried him around all day and no-one knew what she had in her pocket. Bless her.

David and I did a lot of work together. I was working on a film called Treasure Island. It was a German production and was being filmed at Charlestown in Cornwall. It was the second Treasure Island film that year, the first one being for a French company, so lots of work for David, as rats ran everywhere on the boat scenes.

One such day, I was waiting for David to arrive when I received a phone call from him. I asked where he was and he told me that he was about forty miles away. I thought that was fine as filming didn't start until 7:00pm as the shoot was a nighttime one and would run to 6:00am the next morning but he said to me that it wasn't fine, he wouldn't make it in time for filming as his vehicle had actually broken down. I decided that I would go and pick the rats up. David was sure that I would be able to work with them, after all, I had watched him often enough. He certainly had more faith in me than I did.

I had about eight rats in two cages and David had warned me that one of them wasn't very friendly. He had pointed the rat out to me but by the time I got back to the film set I couldn't work out which one was the grumpy one as they all looked the same to me and, with a long night of filming ahead, I had to just pretend that I knew what I was doing, as if I had worked with rats all my life. Believe it or not, I actually had a really good time and became quite attached to the rats and I never found the grumpy one.

38. ALL IN A DAY'S WORK

My children always tried to keep a low profile when I was filming and were quite happy not to get involved, especially the younger one Nick. So you can imagine his shock when, at work at lunch time, when they were all in the hut having their break and most reading newspapers, one of them says to Nick, "Your mum's in the paper." Nick looked up and the bloke was reading The Star. Nick thought, "What had she been up to now?" His mind was working overtime thinking, "She wouldn't, would she?" Nick tried to say that it wasn't his mum but the reply came back, "Oh, yes it is. It says here Pam Weaver of Moreton Valence." Everyone laughed and Nick braced himself. It wasn't that bad really. It was about a film I had been working on with Reese Witherspoon. It involved a frog. The scene was at a dinner table. A young girl had a frog in her hands and she opened her hands to show Reese. The frog jumped on the table then jumped into a large bowl of soup and his next jump was straight down Reese's cleavage. I had to retrieve the frog. Every man that day wanted my job! Luckily the soup was cold. The frog was washed off. The artist was cleaned up and on we went.

39. THEY NAME IT, I GET IT!

A very difficult thing that came my way for one production was the request for hundreds of flies. They were needed to go in a shed of rotting food. The scene was for a door to open and the flies to come swarming out. So, I asked what day this scene was going to be shot. The answer came back that at the moment it was scheduled for such and such a date but that could change. I explained I needed to know precisely the actual date so I could put my plan in action. The only way to get this shot was to get maggots from the fishing shop and hatch them out for the given day (but how long does it take to hatch maggots out?) It really depends on the temperature so I had to do some trial runs and just hope and pray it all came good on the day. I had to go into the dark shed (which was made fly proof) and let out all my flies. On action, the shed door was opened by the artist and with as many cameras as possible set up there would be only one take because after twenty seconds all of the flies would be gone, never to be seen again.

Another scene I had to do was of a bloody battle where there were loads of dead and wounded soldiers, some with terrible flesh wounds, and because they had been there for days, I had to supply maggots and dress the wounds with wriggling maggots. You must, by now, realise when you are an animal supplier, you can get asked for anything. I have worked with camels, cows, bulls, pigs, sheep, donkeys, goats, chickens, ducks, geese, dogs, cats, rats, rabbits, frogs, hedgehogs, spiders (including tarantulas), flies, maggots, lizards and leeches and had tremendous fun, stress and worry along the way. If I was ever asked to do anything which would cause a problem I would give it to another animal agency. I never ever wanted to end my day by not getting the shot they needed. That would get me a bad name and no-one in the film world wants that.

My wranglers from Vanity Fair

LATER LIFE

40. HE WROTE 'BAD DAY'

Dal and I had been working together on a film with Alan Rickman. It had been a short day of filming and we were finished by lunch time. We had arranged to meet our daughter on set at about 3:00pm, not knowing that we would be finished so early, so I rang her and said we would drive to meet her. She was coming from Kings Lynn, Norfolk, and we were somewhere close to Milton Keynes. We travelled the A509 until we got to the A43, Northampton by-pass road. She would be coming down that road so I rang her and told her where we were and at that very moment she was driving over the bridge above us and said "I can see you, I will be there in a minute."

We parked up on some waste land on a disused factory site. There was no footpath, just the busy traffic going by. She arrived and we thought it a good place to have a picnic. We parked our two Land Rovers side by side. She had the three year old twin girls with her and our five year old grandson. We had her older daughter with us, returning her after having a holiday with us. I had one of the twins sat on our tailgate. Grampy, as he was known and adored by his grandchildren, was sat on Lyn's tailgate with his beloved grandchildren. My daughter and I were busy sorting food and drinks when, all of a sudden, our vehicle shot away with our granddaughter still sat on the tailgate. As the vehicle swung down the kerb and onto the main road, all the food, cups and everything flew across the road. Poppy, our granddaughter, was hanging onto the ratchet strap shouting, "Mummy." My daughter was now running after the vehicle shouting for Poppy to jump. That brave little soul rolled onto her tummy, still holding onto the strap, dangled her legs over the tailgate and let go. She rolled and rolled across the tarmac and, by a miracle, no cars hit her. My daughter was with her, cradling her in her arms. The traffic came to a standstill. Poppy was covered in grazes but there was nothing broken. The ambulance came and they spent about an hour with us. Everyone was in shock. People who lived on the opposite side of the road brought us tea and blankets. The ones most badly affected by it all were my husband and grandson, according to the doctor. He told me they needed watching. As for Poppy, she was as bright as a button and talking away as usual, telling everyone that a nasty man stole Grampy's car. The police were on the scene within minutes. A woman who had been waiting to pull out on the opposite side of the road said she saw the whole thing. She said a young lad, who stood in a bush on the opposite side of the road, ran across, almost getting hit by a car, jumped into our vehicle and drove off. My husband would always take the keys out of the ignition and put them in the consol. A man came back to us and said he had followed the vehicle for about five miles but then lost it. The police took statements. We were told that on the opposite side of the road, behind the houses, was a travellers' site and it was a silly place to stop. Although we couldn't say if the man who stole our car was from that site or not, as he was never caught. Anyway, we had no vehicle so I rang our vehicle breakdown service only to be told that they couldn't help us because we didn't have a vehicle for them to recover. It was not a very good situation to be in. My daughter had to drive two hours in the opposite direction to us with herself and four young children still all in shock, and we had to get someone to come and pick us up. In the end my daughter's lovely partner drove to us, making sure his beloved children were okay and then he drove us all the way home.

My husband always had a little notebook by the side of his armchair that he wrote in. Later, when I was reading his notes, I saw that he had just wrote "BAD DAY." A man of few words but I knew how he was feeling. That day I lost so much: my phone with three to four hundred contact numbers, my autograph book with everyone's autograph in, my filming business briefcase and so much more. My husband's vehicle was brand new. It was his pride and joy and his private domain where he would keep his personal bits and pieces. I had no idea what he kept in his little hideaways. My granddaughter had lost all her best and new clothes that her godmother had bought her at Badminton, and her Easter project that she had done for school. Her mobile phone was in her bag which had also been in the vehicle. Her phone rang when you dialled her number. It was our sure hope of getting the vehicle back. Apparently, they hide the vehicle somewhere in case it's got a tracker on it and if no-one turns up to claim it they then dispose of it, one way or another, so if we tracked the phone we would find our vehicle. The police would not trace the phone because it would cost too much money and no-one had died. My oldest granddaughter's partner was a businessman with a large mobile telephone contract and so he approached them. They said they were not allowed to trace telephones but would put up the money for the police to do it. For five days the phone rang each time we rang it. It was so frustrating as no attempts were made to trace the phone to find the car.

41. AT WORLD'S END

Eight days after that awful day we were due to go on our annual holiday with about forty other local farmers and our very best friends, Dave and Beryl.

My husband loved this holiday and really looked forward to it. We did consider not going but I thought it would do him good to get away. The evening of our first day there he said he had indigestion caused by fresh onions that he had enjoyed for lunch. We all met in the evening to go to dinner. We went to the dining room and he decided he would go for a walk and join us later. I said I thought that was probably the best thing for him to do. I went to get a bottle of wine and when I came back he was gone. I never saw him again. We all spent all evening looking for him and then one of our gang heard that a man had collapsed along the sea front. Reception confirmed that was correct and that the man had been taken to hospital. I asked for a taxi to the hospital and went and packed a bag to take with me. Time went by so slowly and nothing was happening, then I started to panic and was told a rep. would have to see me. Eventually two reps walked towards me and said, "Mrs. Weaver, can we see you in a private room?" I knew that instant that he was dead and turned to Beryl and said, "He's dead." I was numb. Beryl and Dave were crying and I was comforting Beryl. I was then taken to the hospital morgue to identify him. I was still numb. It was awful. My worst nightmare ever.

The next fourteen hours, Dave and Beryl never left my side. We went to see where it happened and laid flowers on the spot. I had meetings with officials, Dave and Beryl in floods of tears and me trying to comfort them, saying it will be alright. The travel company offered to fly me home but I said I would wait and take my husband home with me, and anyway, our friends Dave and Beryl needed me. It was early evening and I went back to my room and found a note under my door. I was reading the lovely caring thoughts and all of a sudden I crumbled into a sobbing, useless mess. The sobbing didn't stop for hours. Dave and Beryl moved into my room and I cried myself dry. I kept in touch with my children and it was decided it was best if I travelled home with all my friends. I was determined I wasn't going to spoil their holiday, as all being farmers, they all had the summer's work waiting for them. Every day there were forms to fill out and papers to sign. Dal was being transferred to Istanbul and flown to Heathrow but no-one knew when.

Finally the day came for us to leave. While waiting to enter the airport I had a phone call saying, "We need to see you." I said I was just about to go through the check-in. I was told not to go through and to wait for a call back. Panic stations. Then the phone rang again and they said it was okay, they would sort it. So we stood in the check-in queue and that's when it happened. I had a case belonging to someone who wasn't there and I couldn't take it with me. We tried to explain what had happened, that Dal had died, but I had his ticket, passport and case to go back to England. They got officials to see us and there were lots of phone calls and eventually we were allowed to get on board. I was home at last and the reality of what had happened kicked in. It was like a bad dream. Our children were devastated, all trying to cope with it in their different ways. I rang my friend Charlie the undertaker, who took over the whole situation but there was not a lot he could do until the body arrived and had been transported to Gloucester mortuary.

My husband had died in Turkey on the 20th of May. We had been married for almost fifty years. I felt as if my world had ended. The funeral was arranged for the 12th of June. It was a Saturday and it was going to be a celebration of his life. He was one of the most liked people you could ever meet. He was to be taken to his final resting place from his beloved farm onto the A38 and down the lane that leads to our local church. His last journey was on a lovely old hay cart pulled by his friend's horse, Charlie. The cart was brought to the farm. Our friend Abbie and her family came early to decorate it with flowers. Most people parked in a field at the farm, ready to walk behind the cart. The A38 was closed for us to enter from the farmyard, lead by Charlie the undertaker, then Charlie the Horse, lead by Harold, my husband's friend and neighbour and then followed by the grandchildren carrying baskets of rose petals. We requested that it be family flowers only but people could bring a rose from their garden. It was Danny's favourite flower, especially if it smelled nice.

The lane was filled with people. It took forever to try and get everyone into the church. The doors that were usually kept shut were opened up in an effort to include everyone in the service. It was a lovely service. Our son-in-law gave a heart-warming eulogy to which he finally had everyone laughing. A very embarrassed neighbour's mobile phone kept ringing, a friend sang a solo and dear Eileen read the lovely poem, The Dash by Linda Ellis. The vicar, Richard, gave his address and made a point of saying how much Danny loved his family and, looking straight at me, saying how much he truly loved me. He was carried to his final resting place by his two sons, one of his grandsons, our son-in-law and his two lifelong friends Dave and Dave (Snowy as Dal called him). It was very close to the field edge where our cattle grazed and during the internment the fence behind the vicar kept cracking as the heads of our cattle peered over.

Everyone was invited back to the farm. We never ever expected so many people. There were close to five hundred people there and we had only told the caterers about three hundred. Luckily, lots of friends had brought homemade cakes.

I went to bed happy and content, knowing that he would have approved of his final celebration that we had given him. In the morning, as I laid in bed with my thoughts, I looked at the light coming through the curtains (that had a sort of rose pattern on them) and there, looking at me was my beloved Dal and his lovely smiling face. At that moment my daughter came in with a cup of tea for me. I said "Quick Lyn, can you see Dad in the curtain?" She couldn't see him. I never took my eye off him and told her to put her head on my pillow and I would get up and point to the spot. She said, "Yes I can! I can see Dad."

I drew back the curtains thinking I would be able to see him whenever I wanted to but it didn't matter how hard I looked, I never saw him again. Thinking about it, I draw such comfort from that image. I tell myself it was his way of telling me he liked and approved of what we had done and that gave me real peace of mind to carry me on.

I used to visit his grave every day, as I always walked through the churchyard to check the cattle. One morning, when I arrived at the church, all of our cattle were in the churchyard, mostly around Dal's grave. They were either laying down or just standing, chewing their cud. I could not believe the sight that beheld me. In all the years we had grazed that field they had never once gotten into the churchyard. Thinking back, it was one of those days that I wished I had a camera and, yet again, an unexplained moment.

Me and My Dal

42. LIFE AFTER DAL'S PASSING

The following week I was due to go to the Three Counties Show with the Dexters. The entries had been made and paid for back in early April. My husband had worked hard getting them ready for the show, so I felt it would be a tribute to him to go and show them or all his hard work would have been wasted. So, I asked the show society for extra space and set up a lovely display of photos of him showing our cattle. I decided I would sell the show cattle as I had no heart to go on showing on my own. By the end of the three-day show they were all sold, including his prize bull. My brother came to visit me at the show on the Saturday. We had a cup of tea and some homemade cake together. We were both in the same boat as he had also lost his wife some years earlier. We lived quite close and he was a frequent visitor to the farm. He and my husband got on really well and now he was my rod. The next day, Sunday, was the last day of the show and after the grand parade we were allowed to go home. I arrived home quite late that evening, very tired but happy. All of my friends had come to see me over the three days. They had all enjoyed a cup of tea or coffee and, of course, a piece of homemade cake, as was my usual custom at the show.

I was now back home, done and dusted, as we say, when the phone rang. It was my eldest son, Martin, telling me that my brother Burton was in hospital. He'd had a brain haemorrhage and it was only a matter of time and did I want to go and sit with him at the hospital. Burton's own son, Scott, was with him and Martin was going to sit with Scott for support. I said, "no" as I just couldn't face any more. He died later that night. My husband died on the 20th of May and my brother on the 20th of June, only one week after my husband's funeral. I was devastated. Life was being so cruel and it was becoming so hard to stay positive. His funeral came and went and everyone kept saying time was a great healer. I concentrated on the farm. My youngest son Nick was taking care of the manual side of the farm even though he had a full time job. He did the hay making and all the tractor work for me. We let the sheep go as he found them hard work. I agreed we couldn't keep everything and I went along with his wishes. We soon worked things out and we made a good team.

I wasn't eating properly so by autumn it was suggested that I cook Nick an evening meal while he did the work outside. This way I got a meal as well. I think my daughters had a lot to do with this idea, but it worked and soon I was eating and feeling better. Christmas came and we all spent the Christmas period at the farm. My husband loved Christmas. We all went down to his grave in the afternoon of Christmas Day and sang carols around his grave and Lily, the eldest granddaughter, played the clarinet. It was lovely. The children also left Grampy some chocolate coins covered in gold foil saying, "Grampy's favourite chocolates." The following day they went down to visit him, and came back home saying that Grampy had eaten one of the chocolate coins but only half and had wrapped it back up. Rosie said, "You know chocolate makes Grampy sneeze, so he can only eat half at a time." We all laughed and agreed with her. Oh how they missed and love their beloved Grampy.

The filming by now had gradually faded out. The film I was doing had finished and the T.V. work had come to an end. I didn't take on any fresh contracts as there was no way I could be away from the farm for long periods of time. I went to visit my grandchildren in Norfolk as much as possible but the drive was hard and they didn't like me doing it on my own, so I mainly stayed at home checking and feeding my animals and spending my evenings in front of the log fire, mainly nattering on the telephone.

43. A NEW TEAM

Spring was coming and there was no showing to look forward to. I was beginning to regret selling the show team after Dal had died. Eileen, who loved to come with me when showing the Dexters, suggested that we went to the Three Counties Show as usual and take some calves with us. She said everyone would be looking for me and their cup of tea. In the end it made sense. We wouldn't win but we would be there and, after all, I was a life member of the show, so a pity to waste that.

So that was the start of a new team of animals and we are still at it, but now winning cups and trophies that we first won thirty-two years ago. I know I am getting too old for it but I now have one granddaughter, Charlotte, who is really good and keen and I think she has got some really good teachers in myself and Eileen.

Me and Eileen in our fun t-shirts

I trust I will still have a few more years of showing in front of me. I like nothing better than showing off my magical little Dexters to interested people, after all, it's a subject that has been with me for forty years. Eileen, my trusted true friend, has been as enthusiastic as me and my constant stock mate for thirty-five years and now we have our young apprentice,

Charlotte, one of my many granddaughters, who lives close to me and is as keen as mustard and, of course, young blood and can keep going longer than us two. Between us we make the perfect team. Long may we reign.

Me with Jason Bennett back in the 1980s

44. OF BULLS AND BULLIES

On reflection, I have enjoyed life to the full and have always put all of my energy and enthusiasm into whatever I have been involved in, be it my marriage, bringing up our four children, fostering, running our home and farm, breeding and showing cattle, all of the filming and of course being a Grandmother to our eight wonderful Grandchildren.

I am pleased to say that each phase of my life has brought me much pleasure and satisfaction of a job well done. I have no regrets and if I was given my life over again I would not change a thing. A couple of people have let me down over the years. That is how life is sometimes and you soon learn who your true friends are.

It is with a sad heart that I write this chapter. As you may have experienced yourself at some point in your life, no matter where you go or what type of job you do, there are always a few people who, for no good reason, try to make problems for you. After having Dexters in my life for over forty years (and I am still devoted to the lovely little creatures) and through no fault of the Dexters (or myself for that matter) I have received some very unfair treatment.

As I said earlier in the book, when my Dal died I sold my show team and during the following spring I regretted it so I decided to start another show team up. I only had young calves for that season but the following season they were a year older and looking well and I was looking forward to the shows. I had a very nice young bull and we went to the Bath & West show with him and three other females. On show day he was placed third which was really good for a young bull in a senior class. I was over the moon and it was obvious he would soon be a winner as it was our third show that season and he was being very well placed. Then came the bang! The chief cattle steward and the vet came to see me, saying someone had complained that my bull had ringworm and that I had put boot polish on it to try and hide it. They asked if I would mind if they inspected my animal. I told them it was fine and to help themselves. The vet took a white tissue out of his pocket and wiped around the bull's eye. The tissue was perfectly clean so he tried again, rubbing harder and still the tissue remained as clean as a whistle. He then looked at the bull's eye. The bull had an old injury over his eye which he kept rubbing whenever given a chance to do so. The vet said he didn't think it was ringworm and told me to get him checked over with my own vet when I returned home. So, I did as I was asked and when I got home, my vet came to check him. It was definitely not ringworm and the vet gave me a certificate to say so. The vet and myself had a chat about the bull rubbing himself and we decided the cause was that I was giving him too much barley and flake maize and it was over heating his blood and causing him to itch.

I went to my next show which was the Royal Cornwall show. The troublesome exhibitor was not there fortunately, no-one mentioned the eye and we had a lovely peaceful show.

The next show was the Three Counties. Unfortunately the troublesome exhibitor was at this one and once again the show vet came to see me and said there had been a complaint made against me and my bull and could he check my bull over. Once again I allowed the vet to do what was asked and after a close and careful inspection he said that he didn't think it was ringworm. I said to the show vet, "That's good, my vet will be pleased about that because he gave me a certificate to say just that!" The vet then asked if he could have that certificate to photocopy. When he brought it back he asked if I would pin a copy on my show box which I did, thinking that I could now maybe enjoy the show once more.

The next day we had our classes. Everything went well and my bull won his class. No judge had ever questioned his mark above his eye and he had been in front of four senior judges now which made the whole situation quite ridiculous. Well, that evening, when I was quietly waiting by my cattle, to join the other exhibitors to go to the stock man's dinner party, I was approached by the said 'fly in the ointment' who was very abusive and shouted at me, saying that I was too old for showing and that I should stay home and do my knitting. I was quite alone so I had no witnesses. I was very shaken and quite taken back. I remember asking myself, "Whatever next?"

When we came back from the evening's party, the certificate had been ripped off my show box. The next morning I put another one on. On the last day of the show I was again confronted by the vet and the chairman of the Dexter Cattle Society (DCS). He said that he had been ordered to take hair and skin samples from my bull. I was again very upset but said for him to help himself. When the results came back, as I suspected as much, they were negative. He did not have ringworm.

I thought that was the end of the

bullying that I had had to endure over the past six weeks but, no, it only got worse after that. I received a letter from the DCS stripping me of everything. I had been a judge for twenty or so years. They took that off me. I had been a Field Officer Adviser forever. They took that from me and they said I could never hold any official status within the DCS. The only thing they could not take from me was my life membership. They said that the reason they had done this, was because I had shown an animal that showed signs of ringworm but it was only one person who ever said that my bull had ringworm and, without any doubt at all, he never ever had it.

So after forty years of pure dedication to the DCS this was the way they chose to treat me, a loyal member and one who has been presented with the President's Trophy for services to the society.

This all happened to me while I was still trying to come to terms with the loss of my husband. The bullying and victimization I had to endure resulted in me rupturing my small intestine and almost cost me my life. At the time I was trying to fight my corner but I was just coming up against a brick wall and it was making me so ill that I gave up trying to get justice and an apology. I will never give up on my lovely little cattle and hopefully one day I will get an apology from the DCS and that 'fly in the ointment' that caused me such pain and suffering.

45. GRANDCHILDREN

And now to finish on a happier subject, my grandchildren! I have eight wonderful grandchildren.

There's Martin's two; Harvey, who is a very keen football player just like his Dad was, and Saffron, who is a brilliant rower and is winning many medals for her school.

Then, there's Belinda's four; Lily, who is a very talented young event horse rider, Monty who, like his father and Grampy, is totally mad about tractors, and our two youngest granddaughters, Poppy and Rosie, the twins. They are totally pony mad. Hunting is their greatest love and, just like their mother, they are a fantastic pair of girls.

There's also Louisa's two; Harry, who is the eldest of the grandchildren. He worshiped his beloved Grampy and has followed in his footsteps and is working for the same plant company that both his Dad and Grampy worked for and, I am pleased to say, he lives with me. Then there is Charlotte. She also is horse mad. She is at agricultural college and, I am glad to say, lives close to me so she is able to come showing the cattle with me.

All in all I am a very lucky Grandmother and I appreciate all they do for me and I am only sorry they didn't have their Grandfather around a few years longer while they were growing up and maturing into acceptable young persons. The twins were only three when he was taken from us all. It's not been easy but, eight years on, we are still here as a united family.

I did a "Desert Island Disc" for a radio station many years ago and one of my three records was "United We Stand" (divided we fall). Me and Dal based our marriage on that and it worked for fifty years and I'm glad to say me and our wonderful children still live by the same code.

Pam Weaver

ABOUT THE AUTHOR

Pam Weaver was born and raised in the Forest of Dean, Gloucestershire. She has led an extraordinary life, rearing four of her own children and fostering countless others.

Her passion is her Dexter cattle. She has served as a Dexter judge and sat on the Dexter Cattle Society council for several years.

Pam's cattle led her into becoming a provider of farm animals for a number of Hollywood films and television productions.

She has been exhibiting her pedigree "Migh" herd of Dexters for forty years and won numerous championships at local and national agricultural shows and is now encouraging her grandchildren to follow in her footsteps. She also gives talks about life with her cattle.

Pam lives on her smallholding in Gloucestershire. This is her first book.

Printed in Great Britain
by Amazon